Transformation from Below?

Ursula Scheidegger

Transformation from Below?
White Suburbia in the Transformation of Apartheid South Africa to Democracy

Basler Afrika Bibliographien 2015

Basler Afrika Bibliographien
Namibia Resource Centre & Southern Africa Library
Klosterberg 23
PO Box 2037
CH-4051 Basel
Switzerland
www.baslerafrika.ch

Cover photo: Radium Beer Hall, Louis Botha Avenue, Orange Grove, August 2013.
Photographer: Ursula Scheidegger

ISBN 978-3-905758-58-0
ISSN 2296-6986

Contents

Acknowledgements

Many people have contributed to this book, and I thank them all for their valuable support.

I am very grateful to Professor Shireen Hassim, who supervised the original PhD thesis, for her expert advice, dedication and time. Shireen was a critical reader, pushing me to give my best, but she was also encouraging and supportive when I needed it. Many thanks go to her.

The Department of Political Studies at the University of the Witwatersrand provided a stimulating intellectual environment and offered many opportunities that made this journey an enriching experience. I thank all of my colleagues at the department, especially Professor Sheila Meintjes and my colleagues at the Political Studies Forum – Thomas Kimaru, Bertha Chiroro, Thomas Blaser, Eddy Mazembo-Mavungu, Fritz Schoon and Scott Timcke.

The Swedish International Development Agency (SIDA) provided valuable and much appreciated funding from their grant "Democracy and Social Capital in Segmented Societies".

My colleagues at the Basler Afrika Bibliographien and the Centre for African Studies at the University of Basel offered opportunities for critical engagement with Africa away from my home in Johannesburg. I am grateful to the Basler Afrika Bibliographien for the opportunity to publish this book and I thank Petra Kerckhoff, Christian Vandersee und Dag Henrichsen for their support, inputs and patience and the constructive and efficient cooperation.

I thank all of my interview partners for their time and effort. Their contributions are an essential part of this study.

My friends around the world have supported me during my studies and the work on my thesis, and I am very grateful to them. Ruth Studer in Bern has always been a supportive friend, ever since we faced the challenges of juggling family life and our professional and personal development as young mothers. Kaethy Schneuwly, Barbara Mueller, Mascha Madoerin and Gabriela Wawrinka in Basel, Gisèle Thijs and Anita Glinzler in Johannesburg, Irmgard Weimer in Maputo, and Michèle Oshima in Boston contributed advice and encouragement. Finally, thanks go to my family: I would not be the person I have become without them. My two daughters Madleina and Sophie were always very supportive, and their encouragement gave me the space to embark on this journey. Words cannot describe the ways they changed my life.

Social Dynamics in Two Formerly White Johannesburg Neighbourhoods. An Introduction

South Africa is an example of a relatively successful transition from an authoritarian regime to a liberal democratic state. Comprehensive change of the political system was attained without the breakdown of law and order, the destruction of institutional capacity or the loss of state control. After the transition, procedural democracy has improved, and economic activity has modestly expanded. Social organisations and networks were important agents in this process; they offered structures of interest aggregation and political mobilisation. In addition, social networks substituted dysfunctional state provision to discriminated population groups. The outcome of the political, economic and social transition was shaped and determined by the resources and opportunities available to the various competing social structures and their embeddedness in the legal, institutional and political context (Boix and Posner 1998, Diani 2001, Evans 1996, Nordlund 1996, Woolcock 1998). In the new political and institutional settings of post-apartheid South Africa, the consolidation of democracy depends on the transformation ability of social groups and networks as well as the state's capacity to address the grievances that prompted transition.

In the context of this book, transformation refers to the adaptation of individuals and social groups to the various changes resulting from the political transition in South Africa. Political and legal equality transforms social hierarchies and the access to power, opportunities and resources. It affects social relations between population groups that used to interact in a context of domination and subordination with specific privileges, rights, opportunities and burdens attached to their respective statuses. Hence, transformation requires previously privileged and disadvantaged population groups to respect one another as equal partners in social interactions and development processes. However, social interactions occur in a context where the various population groups not only have different priorities, demands and concerns, but also where skills, organisational and political experience and access to resources and social networks are unequally distributed due to the legacies of apartheid.

Political transitions are times of opportunity but are also characterised by uncertainty, instability, asymmetric risk and benefit distribution, power vacuums, political mobilisation and high emotions. In South Africa, social movements were not only instrumental in initiating and sustaining the transformation process and offering support structures, they also provided the breeding ground for the new political leadership. The liberation movement generated a sense of solidarity that was enforced by the discontinuities in the daily lives of people engaged in the liberation struggle. Nevertheless, the different social groups and organisations also changed during the liberation struggle and the transition. Strategies for promoting or preventing change varied considerably between population groups and their social networks. The result was either different levels of adaptation, integration and accommodation of the new social order or contestation and rejection of the changes. The first democratic elections marked the end of the political transition, but social relations are affected by the past, so the democratisation did not eliminate systemic and structural inequalities and oppressive social hierarchies (Taylor 2003:354).

Nevertheless, the democratisation process in South Africa changed the relations between the different population groups in a complex and far-reaching way, rearranging structures of power, access to resources and opportunities, social hierarchies and values. Citizens and social groups had to reassess and redefine their roles to engage with the changing political context and the economic, social and psychological adjustments it caused. Not only expectations, concerns and fears with respect to the individual and collective consequences of the transition, but also the capacity to accept or reject the changes varied considerably between and within the different population groups. Organisations and networks were the critical social structures that facilitated the engagement with the collective and personal consequences of the transformation. They enabled or impeded individuals from adjusting to comprehensive change successfully (Steyn 2001:xxi).

Group identity provides meaning and a sense of belonging, both are affected by the social and economic consequences of the transition. Not only has the changing access to power and resources affected levels of influence and control, but the new values and social norms have also transformed the reputation of specific individuals and groups. These changes inform perceptions of relevance and status of individuals and groups in the new social and political context (Steyn 2001:158–162). Within the changing political, economic and social environment, space for resistance was limited, and due to the nature of the transition, improvement and development for some people came at the expense of others. The transformation continues to generate tensions between competing social groups in a context where attitudes and the willingness and capacity to accommodate the transformation consequences vary considerably. In sum, social structures have an ambiguous relationship with transformation. Their spectrum of engagement with comprehensive change ranges from adaptation and integration to exclusion and isolation as well as subversion and destabilisation.

The focus of this book is on the transformation potential of two formerly white residential areas in Johannesburg. In contrast to the political transition, social remnants of the old order not only influence but also maintain asymmetric social interactions, offering social spaces where continuities of the past oppose and obstruct change. Accordingly, social and political processes at the micro-level in formerly white neighbourhoods provide insights into the transformation capacity of individuals and social groups as well as the nature and scope of social tensions and conflict.

Norwood and Orange Grove in Johannesburg are the neighbourhoods selected for this study because of their common history and interdependence. Their shared history starts at the beginning of the 20th century, long before the rise of the apartheid regime in 1948. In addition, since the abolishment of the Group Areas Act and in particular in the last decade, both neighbourhoods experienced significant demographic changes. Hence, they provide insights into social dynamics and coping strategies in response to the consequences of racial integration, socio-economic challenges and limited means of control of a formerly privileged population. The engagement with the consequences of the transition occurs in a context where values, social norms and standards, social hierarchies and access to power and resources are in a state of flux.

The South African transition, the subsequent transformation of social hierarchies, the distribution of power and opportunities, the usefulness of social resources and the utilities that emanate from relations with other people or groups also affect the access and utilisation of urban space. The end of apartheid and racial segregation resulted in a comprehensive transformation of the social environment in South Africa's cities. A number of formerly white neighbourhoods experienced changes in the demographic composition of the population and levels of homogeneity. The development of neighbourhoods is beyond the control of individuals: neighbours depend on mutual cooperation to respond to changes that are often random, increase impermanence and create transience in social interactions. Space is essential for human relations and has specific symbolic meaning and emotional significance (Foster 2005:498). Nevertheless, visions and normative standards of an ideal neighbourhood differ between the various population groups. Despite the distinct history and reputation of specific neighbourhoods that tend to outlive transformation, residents have only limited means to influence or prevent the influx of newcomers, which contributes to uncertainty, conflict and feelings of powerlessness.

In South Africa, perceptions of different racial and ethnic groups were shaped by history, state ideologies, worldviews, socialisation, tradition, personal experiences and emotional aspects such as perceived threats or prejudices. These experiences influence social interactions and levels of cooperation. In a segmented society such as South Africa, not only fault lines but also collective reputation, social stigma and social barriers have developed over time. In addition, levels of trust and the disposition to interact with people from a different social-cultural context are based on culture, tradition, internalised behavioural patterns, habits and personal experiences.

The impact of the history of racial segregation is still visible in Johannesburg's settlement patterns, and has influenced the historical growth of neighbourhoods and communities. In Norwood and Orange Grove, homogeneity and low levels of conflict affected social dynamics and associational life, resulting in the development of a distinct identity. During the apartheid years, the control of space was a central foundation of the political and social order and a significant element of securing state capacity (Robinson 1998). Hence, the apartheid state rigorously imposed regulations that are not only reflected in residence patterns but also left little choice for the non-white population through forced removals, relocations and a system of brutal control. Today, perceptions of acceptable behavioural standards and measures of social control are still influenced by the apartheid experience. As a consequence, there is a tendency to problematise and criminalise behaviour that is accepted in public spaces of more liberal societies (Du Toit 2003).

The different Johannesburg urban development frameworks promote urban integration as a shared common good. This approach not only fails to engage with conflictual views, priorities and development goals, but also overlooks the unequal distribution of power and resources of the different stakeholders engaged in urban neighbourhoods (Pieterse 2003:136). At the micro-level of urban neighbourhoods, the degree of tension, conflict, access to power and access to resources informs social interactions, coping mechanisms and strategies for integrating, confronting or preventing transformation.

After the 1994 elections, decentralisation and local government reform became a central aspect of the democratisation process. Local politics is considered relevant to the lives of individuals and groups because local government is closest to the people and their concerns and demands. Moreover, after the experience of an authoritarian state during apartheid, the emphasis on civil society, participation and decentralised political structures is understandable as a means of controlling excessive government interventions that potentially interfere with personal and collective opportunities and choices. Participatory political structures motivate civic engagement and provide structures for the involvement of the citizenry. Social networks enable and facilitate cooperation and collective action. The cooperation between the population, local government and the administration improves the communication between the population and political structures. Participatory processes increase the responsiveness to local demands and concerns, ensuring that political decisions, policies and service provisions are based on the needs of the citizenry. In participatory local political structures, the presence and nature of social networks influence the quality of cooperation between citizens and local government, thereby affecting governance and government performance.

The ward is the most decentralised political structure in the municipality of Johannesburg, the ward councillors are elected during municipal elections. Councillors are assisted by the ward committee, elected by ward residents and ideally representing the different population groups and geographical areas of the ward. The 2001 Census offers an overview of the racial composition of residents in the two local government wards in which Norwood and Orange Grove are located. In this study, references to the different racial groups are presented in the terms commonly used in South Africa.

In Ward 73, where Norwood is located, population numbers are as follows:

Africans	Coloureds	Indians	Whites
7374	367	1139	18427

In Ward 74, where Orange Grove is located, population numbers are as follows:

Africans	Coloureds	Indians	Whites
11610	428	825	18053

(based on Census 2001, Statistics South Africa)

In connection with decentralisation, local government reform and participatory structures in the local polity, the concept of social capital became popular in debates on the South African democratisation process. Social capital facilitates cooperation and through cooperation in community structures social capital is generated and sustained. The *White Paper on Local Government* explicitly states: "All over the world, communities must find ways to sustain their economies, build their societies, protect the environment, improve personal safety (in particular for women) and eliminate poverty. There is no single correct way to achieve these goals. National frameworks and support from other levels of government are critical, but cities, towns and rural communities are increasingly having to find within themselves ways to make their settlements more sustainable. This requires trust between individuals and open and accommodating relationships between stakeholders. Local government has a key role to play in building this kind of social capital – this sense of common purpose – to find local solutions for increased sustainability" (White Paper 1998:41).

Robert Putnam initiated the social capital debate in his seminal book *Making Democracy Work: Civic Traditions in Modern Italy*, where social capital is considered an important aspect of social dynamics, associational life and the quality of civic engagement. Especially intriguing was Putnam's theoretical framework linking successful democratic dispensations to levels of social capital. According to Putnam, social capital is intrinsic to social functioning because it enables people to cooperate and achieve a common purpose. Social networks, associations or interest groups have an important function in democratic dispensations by promoting concerns and demands of individual citizens, by stimulating debate and by eventually exerting pressure on government. Hence, for Putnam social capital is the variable explaining democratic institutional performance and the essential factor for making democracy work (Putnam 1993). Consequently, the concept of social capital gained popularity in South African debates and academic writing on democratisation, local government, social cohesion and community development based on Putnam's conceptualisation of social capital and its potential benefits.

In contrast to Putnam's understanding of social capital as a reflection of attitudes and a specific political culture, the concept is also used as a structural variable and was thus introduced by Bourdieu in 1972. As a structural variable, social capital is a resource linking the individual to networks of relations and the opportunities membership in a particular group provides (Bourdieu 1972, Bourdieu and Wacquant 1996). Consequently, structural and relational aspects of social capital explain inequalities and limitations of social assets, because networks differ enormously in terms of power structures and the resources they are able to access (Foley and Edwards 1999:162-165). The social, economic and political context critically shapes the space for civic engagement, where norms, values and attitudes emerge from a political, social and economic environment where benefits and burdens are unequally distributed and where individual behaviour and sociability can only be fully understood in the broader societal context. The utility emanating from social relations and networks is further influenced by the access to power, the extent of inequality and levels of conflict. Moreover, the quality of social capital depends on the purpose for which it is used. Human beings depend on social relations to respond to daily challenges and to achieve something, hence social capital works at different levels from family and kinship to neighbourhoods and cities. As a structure of social support, individuals rely on human relations to address and resolve daily challenges and problems. In contrast, social capital can also serve to achieve something and increase personal influence and leverage due to personal relations or membership in a particular group (Briggs 1997:111–112).

Transformation is a latent source of contention, especially in a context of high levels of poverty and inequality and the challenge of racial integration. In a neighbourhood where resources, opportunities and burdens are unequally distributed, decentralisation and participatory structures may prevent change as powerful individuals or social organisation potentially dominate local communities or resort to alternatives that could undermine the public good such as the growth of private facilities. People from very different socio-economic contexts have different priorities and not much in common. Moreover, there is no incentive for privileged groups to change arrangements that benefit them, so they try to undermine processes of transformation

Overview

This book is an edited and extended version of my PhD thesis. Local associations and political organisations in Norwood and Orange Grove that engage with the local polity were included in this study, namely the Community Police Forum, residents' and business associations, immigrants' organisations and political parties. These voluntary organisations facilitate interest aggregation, have a certain representative function and are potentially useful for the mobilisation of citizens. Ward councillors and ward committees are the only elected institutions included in this study. The various ways in which community organisations interact with the government and the public administration offer insights into the demands, concerns and aspirations of the population. They also reveal the extent of tensions and conflict between different social structures, their access to resources, the distribution of power and bargaining leverage and the resulting hierarchies among different local stakeholders. The racial composition of the different community structures reflects levels of integration.

Schools are included because of the different social structures that develop around schools. The four schools in the two neighbourhoods provide insights into levels of racial integration and parental support structures. They also indicate their embeddedness in the neighbourhood and their ability to act as facilitators of neighbourhood sociability. Finally, institutions of faith are discussed because they are the most prominent civil society structure in South Africa, contributing to the vibrancy of social life. Membership in institutions of faith is voluntary, they are separated from the state and usually financially independent. The study includes different Christian denominations as well as the Muslim and Jewish community, which are the two other significant religious groups in the geographical area of this study. The field work was conducted between 2006 and 2008. However, I revisited the two neighbourhoods and conducted further fieldwork in 2013 and 2014 in order to assess changes and the extent of transformation.

The first chapter discusses social dynamics and engages with the concept of social capital and its relevance and usefulness in the context of this study. The legacies of the apartheid past – in particular the extent of inequalities, the politicisation of race and the high incidence of crime and violence – influence social dynamics in Norwood and Orange Grove. Moreover, social and political interactions occur in a context of pervasive value changes and rearranged patterns of access to power that affect individual and collective spaces of agency. Structural and systemic inequalities perpetuate oppressive social relations and affect personal well-being and perceptions of justice and fairness. In decentralised political structures there is the problem of representation, especially in a context of high levels of inequality. As local structures depend on the engagement of the community there is the danger that well connected, active and articulate community members dominate local processes and potentially promote particular interests. Moreover, there is a tendency that government and administrative structures engage with highly visible and dominant local individuals or groups, privileging them at the expense of more informal and less visible groups.

The second chapter discusses aspects of the South African transition that are relevant to social dynamics at the micro-level of local politics. The South African transition and political negotiations were influenced by different agents with conflicting visions of the new South Africa. Networks and social resources were critical during this process. They positioned the different groups and factions of the liberation movement by influence, bargaining leverage and access to power and paved the way for the emergence of the new political leadership in a context of high expectations and limited resources. Challenges to democratic consolidation are the extent of inequality and poverty, the alienation between different population groups, the politicisation of race and the high incidence of crime. Particular political and social dynamics emanate from the dominance of the African National Congress (ANC) and affect the quality of politics and levels of responsiveness, transparency and accountability.

The third chapter debates public space and its influence on the spatial environment of local politics and social dynamics in the two neighbourhoods. Perceptions of safety, security and order critically shape attitudes to public space in a context where opinions regarding desirable levels of security and acceptable behaviour vary between the different social groups. In formerly white neighbourhoods, the inability to assert control contributes to uncertainty; thus conflict informs social and political dynamics and measures of control and surveillance in a context where power and resources are unevenly distributed.

The fourth chapter presents different community and political organisations and associations in Norwood and Orange Grove. It includes the Community Police Forum (CPF), the two residents' associations, the Norwood Orchards Residents' Association (NORA) and the Orange Grove Residents' Associations, and the two most active political parties in the neighbourhood, the African National Congress (ANC) and the Democratic Alliance (DA). The two ward councillors and members of both ward committees are the only elected institutions included in this study and interviews were conducted with representatives. Moreover, the business associations along Grant Avenue as well as the two immigrants' associations of the Italian and Greek communities were approached. The focus of the interviews was on the activities, programmes and priorities of the different community structures and the challenges, problems and difficulties they face. In addition, the quality of communication and cooperation with political institutions and the City of Johannesburg administration were assessed.

The fifth chapter discusses the transformation of the education sector using fieldwork in the four Primary Schools located in Norwood and Orange Grove. It looks at the role of education in empowering formerly discriminated population groups, and the correlation between levels of education, citizenship and civic engagement. Education has a critical role in empowering people, increasing social capital, fostering social and political engagement, reducing inequalities and contesting traditional perceptions of gender roles or the use of violence to address conflicts. Changing admission policies influence the social environment of schools and contacts to the community and neighbourhood, which impacts on sociability in Norwood and Orange Grove.

The sixth chapter discusses religious institutions because a significantly higher percentage of South Africans are members of a religious community than of any other civil society structure. Religion is often considered the glue of society and associated with high levels of quality relations. Nevertheless, religious communities do not necessarily engage with the state nor with local political institutions. Places of worship offer space were people from different population groups can meet. The emphasis on equality of most religious institutions provides interesting insights into responses to inequality, racial discrimination and gender relations. The secularisation of the state and the promotion of new values potentially create conflict with religious morals, values, beliefs and perceptions of the social order. The various institutions of faith employ different strategies to engage with the challenges of value changes and the new social order. The Christian, Jewish and Muslim communities are included in this chapter.

The seventh chapter assesses the changes between the first phase of fieldwork (2006 to 2008) and the second phase (2013 and 2014). It follows up on projects and assesses the levels of implementation. The different community institutions were revisited, most of them still struggle with low numbers of citizens willing to get involved. Moreover, the degree of racial integration has not improved in a context where according to the 2011 census demographics have changed and the number of non-white residents living in the two neighbourhoods exceeds the number of white residents.

The eighth chapter analyses the research findings and the effects of the South African transition on social relations and networks. In contrast to the political transition, continuities of the past in the social sphere perpetuate asymmetric relations and offer space for the obstruction of change. Thus, democratisation does not eliminate systemic and structural inequalities, oppressive social hierarchies or the legacies of apartheid. In the two local communities, the unequal distribution of power, burdens, access to opportunities and access to resources influences social dynamics. There is a danger that powerful individuals and organisation dominate local politics and potentially undermine democratic processes as there are little incentives to change arrangements that benefit them. Nevertheless, democratic consolidation in South Africa depends on the one hand on the extent to which social organisations and networks are willing to address the problems, grievances and hardships that are consequences of apartheid; on the other hand, in this context of pervasive inequalities state capacity is important in order to limit and constrain powerful local groups from dominating local politics.

1 Social Dynamics and the Concept of Social Capital

Introduction

Following the wave of democratisations in the 1980s and 1990s in Eastern Europe and the Global South including South Africa, discussions on the necessary requirements to sustain liberal democratic regimes became prominent. Approaches focused on civil society, social dynamics and state-civil society relations to assess political processes and to promote good governance and government accountability. In South Africa, decentralisation, local government reform and participatory political structures became central aspects of democratic consolidation. After the experience of the authoritarian state during apartheid, the emphasis on participation and civil society engagement was considered to ensure responsiveness to popular demands and grievances and thus safeguard democracy. Nevertheless, in a context of structural and systemic inequalities and a divisive history, the question of representation and interest articulation is more complicated. The South African transition has affected social hierarchies and access to power and resources but at the same time continuities of the past maintain asymmetric social interactions that obstruct change. Moreover, social interactions occur in a context where people have different priorities and expectations and where political and organisational experience and access to power and opportunities are unequally distributed. The transition continues to generate tensions because due to the legacies of apartheid development and improvement for some people comes at the expense of others.

Social network and community organisations have a critical role in resolving dilemmas of collective action and offer structures of interest aggregation, representation, public debate, mobilisation and interaction with government institutions. Local networks facilitate communication and serve as structures of social control. Nevertheless, not everyone involved in community organisation is interested in politics and not all social networks have a political impact or are well connected to political structures; access to power and resources varies considerably between social networks and between members in specific groups. Moreover, even in prominent community organisations social relations occur not only in formal settings. The space of agency and manoeuvring in the informal sphere of social relations equally determine levels of social capital and the resources individuals gain from contacts to or affiliations with other people and networks. In informal relations boundaries between the personal and formal are blurred and shifting and social interactions are less transparent and beyond measures of social control or obligations of accountability. In this context of formal and informal relations social capital is an individual resource that eventually also benefits specific interests or social groups.

The Social Capital Debate – Social Capital as a Collective or Individual Resource

As already argued in the introduction, Putnam re-introduced social capital and the concept became prominent for assessing levels and the quality of cooperation and trust in local communities. Moreover, the link between social capital and democratic institutional performance was deemed to explain how democracies work (Putnam 1993). Putnam managed to move away from and ignore earlier social capital debates for example from Bourdieu's theoretical development and conceptualisation of social capital that centred on individuals and small units as well as on the benefits and constraints arising for individuals and families through their social connections and interactions with others (Portes 2000:1–2). According to Portes, Putnam initiated the "conceptual stretch" from individuals to a collective asset with collective benefits emanating from it. This transition from an individual to a collective resource was never explicitly theorised, and it is the cause of the current confusion about the meaning of social capital and its multifaceted applications. The two meanings of the concept, either as an individual or a collective resource, are potentially incompatible because individual social capital and the benefits of individual social ties may be used to undermine collective social capital and the pursuit of shared objectives (Portes 2000:3–4).

Putnam re-introduced the social capital debate at a time where neo-liberal development strategies, self-reliance and a small state dominated the political and economic agenda. Hence, the introduction of social capital as a collective resource was a convenient strategy to move the focus away from the role of the state to civil society and the local polity (Fine 1999:2). The concept of social capital is attractive to development approaches that minimise or neglect the role of the state and promote reductions in public spending, which explains the popularity of Putnam's approach and the concept's prominence in academic debates (Harriss and De Renzio 1997:920). The focus on social capital and local communities obscures objective structural or systemic problems and prevents adequate government response to these problems that are impossible to resolve on the local level. Decentralised local development does not for instance solve structural problems such as lacking resources, unemployment, poor service provision, skills shortages and deficient infrastructural development (Portes and Landolt 1996:42). In the South African context of widespread poverty and high income inequality the shift from the state to local communities as agents of development is even more questionable because the poor depend disproportionally on the public sector for short-term survival. According to Abedian, effective poverty alleviation and medium to long-term development depend on substantial public sector intervention (Abedian 2003:82). Unlike decentralisation and community-centred development approaches, in developmental states the primacy is on politics because only the state has the capacity, autonomy and power to promote explicit developmental objectives (Leftwich 1995:401, 421).

Due to Putnam's vague conceptualisation of social capital and the circularity of his argument, it is difficult to assess whether social capital enables civic engagement, or civic engagement generates social capital (Harris and De Renzio 1997:922–927). Moreover, there is a lack of analytical differentiation between the cause and effect of social capital (Portes 2000:4) and a confusion and conflation of democracy with governance (Koelble 2003:207). Foley and Edwards stress the unclear relationship between civil society and democratic governance since there are at least two different aspects of civil society with conflicting interests: the first engages with the state, but the second challenges the state (Foley and Edwards 1996:39–40). The example of South Africa's transition clearly shows the ambiguous relationship between civil society and the state, dominant values, and law and order. Putnam avoids engaging with social organisations that challenge dominant political and socio-economic values and neglects the discussion of conflict in the vertical structures of civil society organisations. Moreover, Putnam ignores structural aspects, particularly power relations, within and between organisations and the critical role of dominant organisations and powerful and well-connected individuals in selecting issues for public debate.

Bourdieu used the concept of social capital to develop an analytical tool in his theoretical work to assess personal development and agency in relation to socio-economic context. In contrast to Putnam, Bourdieu considers social capital an individual asset. His discussion of social capital is more complex and his focus is on power, hierarchy, conflict, inequality and the space of agency. Furthermore, the socio-economic, political and institutional context is included as a critical factor that shapes social relations, which is important for a more comprehensive assessment and analysis of social realities in post-apartheid South Africa (Bourdieu 1983, 1988, 2005).

According to Bourdieu social capital is a structural element that is unevenly distributed and facilitates or constrains certain actions. Personal upbringing and the family background determine opportunities and constraints and personal levels of social capital. Moreover, Bourdieu considers family background, particularly socio-economic class, an important element in the reproduction and perpetuation of power structures and social hierarchies that define social practice (Bourdieu 1983, 1988, 2005; Bourdieu and Wacquant 1996). This aspect is important in the South African context with its structural and systemic legacies of apartheid. Hence, Bourdieu's conceptualisation of social capital is relevant and useful in the South African context of enormous structural differences because it allows engaging with conflict, inequality, competition and space of agency and opportunity.

Consequently, social capital is more than an essential element of civil society structures that facilitates coordinated action and reflects a rich and vibrant associational life (McLean et al. 2002:9). Civil society is not a homogeneous entity: it is amorphous, represents a variety of interests, is stratified and has an unequal distribution of power. In South Africa civil society is heterogeneous and includes a multiplicity of different social groups with their varied aspirations and concerns. Due to the extent of inequality, poverty levels and the politicisation of race, civil society is a space of negotiations, conflict and tensions where social resources, social capital and the access to power and opportunities are unequally distributed.

In an environment of conflicting interests and unequal power distribution, the focus on Norwood and Orange Grove – two formerly white residential areas – provides interesting insights into social dynamics and transformation capacity in response to the South African transition and local government reform. In Norwood and Orange Grove, a formerly privileged population group is challenged by changing demographics, increasing heterogeneity and limited means of control. This transformation occurs in a context where values, social norms, social hierarchies, access to power and access to resources have changed dramatically. Neighbourhoods facilitate and depend on social relations that are concerned with the development of their area, because development and the addressing of problems exceed individual agency and the cooperation with other people is imperative. Nevertheless, space of agency, levels of social capital and access to power and resources allow for the development of structures that limit cooperation with the state and sideline population groups with different development priorities. Social and financial capital and the encouragement of public-private partnerships potentially enable the promotion of an agenda that undermines the public good and serves the interests of a minority.

The Role of State and Institutions in Local Communities

A favourable environment for community sociability and the propensity of people to engage with other people or groups depends on fundamental institutional preconditions such as political and civil rights and law and order. Social organisations have an important representative function and facilitate information flows, contact and interactions between different social structures, civil society and the government. Since social organisations differ in terms of size and resources, institutions also have an important function in monitoring and controlling discriminatory practices and favouritism that originate from the unequal position of social networks (Hadenius 2004:55–56). Moreover, the fundamental question arises whether political participation and civic engagement are attractive enough for people to get involved, and which underlying motivational factors stimulate civic mobilisation and participation. According to Steger, the individualism of neoliberal markets and widening inequality levels correspond with the decline of social capital and social engagement, the removal of social control measures and the liberalisation and deregulation of the market. They have all contributed to the destruction of social relations and civic obligations in communities (Steger 2002:265–271). In a context where the primacy is the market, politics are marginalised, in particular representative democratic structures because political decisions based on popular consent might interfere with market efficiency (Butterwegge 2008:14). The diminishing interest in politics and civic engagement are the result of the narrowing political space where debate and political campaigning become increasingly meaningless in the face of the massive growth of corporate power and the finance sector and its domination of the public sphere and social life (Boggs 2002:190–191). Low expectations of influence in local politics, the insignificance of local structures in political processes and the arrogance of governments sidelining popular demands and grievances impact on motivation and efforts to get involved. In South Africa, the fact that people participate in political activities outside of institutionalised politics proves the capacity to overcome the collective action dilemma to engage with the state. However, the current imbalance of power encourages political engagement outside the institutionalised context.

Offe argues that trust in the political system is an important aspect of democracies, which impacts on civic engagement. Political trust is based on institutionalised systems of checks and balances and transparency and accountability. A trustworthy person, especially in a position of political representation, is honest and accountable, behaves in an overt and transparent way and allows for continuous and scrupulous examination by others (Offe 1999:55–57). The erosion of trust in political institutions is a serious threat to democracy, because social integration and political stability in the impersonal, complex environment of the modern state depend on trust in the capacity and impartiality of state institutions. The assurance that strong institutions are consistent, maintain safety and security and enforce the law has significant implications on the disposition of individuals to respect the law, influencing the social environment (Newton and Norris

1999:58–68). Perceptions of fairness and impartiality allow citizens of different political affiliations to believe that government institutions respect all citizens. Furthermore, not only institutional capacity but also normative, moral and ethical standards that inform political processes and practices as well as the behavioural choices of the political representation influence the social attitudes of citizens and their assessments of state capacity. Corruption erodes political trust, destroying human relations and cooperative social practice (Rothstein and Stolle 2003:192–200). Social interactions in communities are therefore influenced by the degree of confidence in a respectful citizenry, state capacity and social norms of civility as well as institutional performance and law enforcement (Offe 2000:4–5, Newton and Norris 1999:67).

Perceptions of the political and social environment, transparency and a system of checks and balances impact on the generation of political trust and are important in the South African context of democratic consolidation. Governments can not only encourage trust relations; more significantly, governments also influence civic behaviour by their own behavioural standards. Corruption has detrimental effects on social relations and civic engagement. The violation of regulations and norms not only by other citizens but also by corrupt government officials affects the confidence in the social order and reduces levels of trust. Furthermore, corrupt practice tends to privilege certain individuals or population groups (Rothstein 2004:125). The disrespect of rights and laws and the violation of social norms, especially by government and political representation impact on social life and civic engagement (Kim 2005:209). Standards of impartiality, fairness, transparency and accountability in the government and its institutions critically influence the quality of the social, economic and political environment that informs social dynamics and sociability (Rothstein and Stolle 2003:194). In a context where people are dissatisfied or suspicious of the state, the government and the way politics is conducted, the emphasis on civic attitudes and political engagement as a means of democratic renewal and political change are unrealistic and ignore the complexity of political processes (Paterson 2000:39).

Finally, the state is not an exogenous factor of civil society and associational activity is embedded in the political, social and economic environment with its challenges and limitations. In this context, not only civic engagement but also shifting alliances, political crisis and divisions between the political elite or electoral competition offer opportunities for community structures to exert pressure on governments, voice grievances, promote demands and influence the quality of politics (Maloney et al. 2000:83–89). Hence, it is not only civic engagement and levels of social capital but also political opportunity structures that shape the interactions between the government and the people, a relevant aspect in the context of limited electoral competition and the dominance of the African National Congress (ANC) in South Africa.

The Impact of Inequality on Local Communities and Civic Engagement

It is of critical importance to pay attention to the social, economic and political context and its distribution of opportunities and burdens that shape the space of civic engagement. Sociability and civic attitudes emanate from this broader societal context and are influenced by perceptions of the integrity of political institutions and the government and the distribution of benefits and constraints. According to Costa and Kahn heterogeneity, in particular income inequality and a high Gini Coefficient, is negatively correlated with levels of civic engagement and levels of cooperation (Costa and Kahn 2001:31–33). In South Africa's society with high levels of inequality, a diversity of interests and a high potential of social conflict, social networks and social capital become an ambiguous resource. Fine argues that the impact of social capital is more complicated in societies that are marred by social conflict. By avoiding questions of power and conflict, Putnam not only neglects the destructive nature of social capital but also the limited influence of social capital on democratic processes (Fine 1999:9, 14). In a context of contestation, powerful actors in civil society are engaged in promoting their own interests. Their position in social and political hierarchies and the different forms of capital determine available resources and the extent of influence and power (Siisiäinen 2000:8–9). Often, access to education and professional development increases social leverage and broadens the range of opportunities, networks and choices. Moreover, the engagement in civil society structures facilitates the expansion of personal networks of clients and patronage (Mosse 2001:29). Finally, there are additional asymmetries in organisational skills, media exposure, political experience and political maturity of individuals and the various civil society groups (Portes 2000:5).

The purpose for which social capital is used is also marginalised, debates centre on benefits and exclude the possibility that social capital can facilitate destructive outcomes. Growing levels of income concentration, the social exclusion of large masses, hopelessness, unbearable levels of crime and violence at the periphery and lacking prospects of decent living conditions contribute to a social environment where people have nothing to lose (Dupas 2001:1–9). Rubio warns of the consequences that arise if formal employment for unskilled labour generates less economic benefits than the informal sector: in other words, if crime is profitable and low-risk because of weak law enforcement agencies. Rubio uses the label "perverse social capital" in the context of economic incentive structures that promote social and economic activities which undermine society and the state because they not only encourage and facilitate illegal activities, but are also embedded in strong social networks that perpetuate this dynamic (Rubio 1997:805-812). In the context of South Africa's crime problem, not only Rubio but also Portes and Stuart Hall are relevant with their focus on contextual aspects of the social environment. Portes argues that common experiences of adversity and opposition to mainstream society generate solidarity in a context of high levels of inequality and the resulting limitations on personal development prospects. This solidarity is the result of exclusion, discrimination, indignity and limited access to resources and anti-social behaviour not only becomes a substitute for lacking opportunities and social recognition, but is also an effective strategy to challenge mainstream society (Portes 1998:17). Subcultures are not only characterised by normative expectations and strong regulations that are rigorously enforced, but also by high levels of bonding social capital as they provide social status that is denied by mainstream society (Hall S. 2002:44).

On the other hand, criminality and social exclusion also affect social bonds in a different way; in South Africa, intolerable levels of crime foster solidarity and mutual support against a "common enemy" (Altbeker 2005:224–225). Negative perceptions of personal realities arising from insecurity and threats have consequences on the quality of social relations and promote high levels of bonding in exclusive groups that offer a sense of safety and belonging. These groups restrict membership, tend to have a positive view on their members or take pride in their community membership but they also stereotype outsiders. In addition, the more people are dependent on each other, the more they divide the social world in categories of "we" and "they". People who view their own demographic group positively send a strong message of exclusivity (Uslaner 1999: 28–32, 124-126). Moreover, in a context of crime and insecurity, spatial arrangements that limit and control access to designated urban areas provide a sense of security. This privatisation of public space is exclusive and increases social interactions among economically more privileged groups at the expense of more inclusive development objectives. Stolle, Soroka and Johnston emphasise the importance of direct contact between members of different population groups in a heterogeneous community. Direct contacts reduce prejudices and clichés, provide interesting social experiences and encourage the accommodation of diversity, the characteristics of modern society (Stolle et al. 2008:58–59)

Inequality and the extent of social leverage is also a result of social location, for example class, gender or minority status. Furthermore, reputation is an important individual or collective asset linked to the degree of recognition that an individual or social group enjoys. Reputation influences the trustworthiness of individuals and impacts on social relations Hence, social groups vary in their structural positions and the value assigned to different aspects of personal and social life determines opportunities and choices (Lin 2001:55, 95, 143–154). Values and social norms influence reputation, authority, significance and importance of individuals and social networks, however, they are not universal but universalised by the dominant culture. (Siisiäinen 2000:14–17). Consequently, values potentially function as ideologies, if they are based on the premise that the underlying social order is natural and not negotiable, and they therefore prevent the exploration of more emancipatory structures (Young 1990:74). This is an important aspect, especially relevant for the South African situation: the ambiguous relationship between dominant values and social transformation.

Conclusion – Is Social Capital a Useful Concept?

Democracies depend on the attitudes, behaviour and values of citizens and their ability to tolerate people from different backgrounds, their flexibility with respect to identity construction, their propensity for civic engagement and their participation in political processes. Nevertheless, the governments and the political and institutional context create the social environment that generates a sense of belonging among the citizenry and the necessary degree of identification with the political community (Offe, 1999, 2000; Kymlicka and Norman 2000:6–8). South Africa has a highly unequal distribution of resources, opportunities and burdens as well as strong hierarchies and a significant potential for social conflict. Limited state capacity reduces constraints on powerful agents, which is reflected in the growing authority of private institutions. Facilities outside the state empower dominant civil society networks and the private sector. This shift of power and authority is especially attractive in the context of the South African transition where access to political power and the state has changed. However, it limits democratisation and the development of a more egalitarian and just society and it prevents the promotion of the public good based on the needs and aspirations of the entire population.

In this context, the reliance on community structures and local networks as promoters of development is problematic, because the qualities of social capital depend on the purpose for which it is used. The South African transition changed access to power and opportunities and rearranged social hierarchies. However, the resilience of asymmetric social relations and patterns of domination in the local social space oppose and obstruct transformation. Limited state capacity has serious consequences in the context of inequalities and decentralised political structures because powerful groups with vested interests dominate local political and social processes. Social capital facilitates their access to relevant and powerful individuals and networks enabling them to promote their particular agenda. Social capital can become the variable undermining democratisation and is hence a useful concept for assessing the unequal distribution of social resources and the access to power and opportunities they provide. Moreover, social capital allows at least to conceptualise the importance of informal, unofficial or concealed social structures, the social interactions that occur behind closed doors and for example are manifest in gate keeping, selective information dissemination or patterns of exclusion. The nature of these informal networks renders it impossible to assess the significance, weight, impact, and consequences they have on local communities. Nevertheless, social capital is the indispensable factor that enables and sustains these networks and the influence they exert.

2 The Challenges of Democratic Consolidation in South Africa

Introduction

The peaceful, controlled transition and democratisation process in South Africa attracted worldwide attention and admiration. The transition was successfully negotiated in a context of enormous individual and collective damages inflicted by the apartheid regime and its social consequences. Despite different perceptions of democracy and the resulting expectations, there was an overarching consensus among all my interview partners included in this study that they valued democracy positively. Nevertheless, there were distinct and conflicting anticipations of the transition process and the new political, economic and social order. In addition, the various population groups were affected by the transition in very different ways. The democratic elections in April 1994 and the inauguration of the first democratically elected government marked the formal end of apartheid. Democratic consolidation is still influenced by the legacies of apartheid, in particular the challenges of extreme inequalities and alienation between the various population groups.

During transitions, social relations and networks are not only critical to initiate and maintain social mobilisation but also enable or constrain actors. Social structures offer support, link the movement to political and economic elites and provide the breeding ground for the new political leadership. Furthermore, the discussion of new ideas, the vision of a transformed society and the modification of moral standards are initiated and circulated (Diani 2001:207–209). Nevertheless, political transitions are unstable, unpredictable and emotionally charged, undermining to a certain extent the viability of state institutions (Przeworski 1995:38). The various organisations involved in the South African liberation struggle had different agendas and conflicting interests. They differentiated themselves in terms of access to power, assets, political experience and influence on the transformation process. Transitions are negotiated in a context of opportunities and limitations, so the question arises whether democratisation is just a regime change or produces a fundamental structural transformation of the state.

People also had different expectations of democracy. In a new democracy, citizens, social networks and the state have to reassess and redefine their roles. In addition, certain socio-economic conditions are required so that people can exercise their rights effectively (Przeworski 1995:35). Taylor argues that the political, social and economic spheres interact and reproduce social identities; they are affected by the continuities of the past and try to locate themselves in the opening spaces of the new social and political order. The transformation of the political system does not modify the asymmetrical living circumstances of the different population groups (Taylor 2003:353–354). The democratisation process is not completed with the first election because the democratisation of the political realm does not mean the democratisation of society. Bourdieu states that domination is not always a direct action imposed on the oppressed but rather embedded in a complex set of relational interactions in a constraining environment that limits the personal space of agency (Bourdieu 1998:31–34).

The political transition had effects on different aspects of social life with contrasting experiences and consequences for the various population groups. Ideologies that informed economic strategies and social transformation were contested. The reconfiguration of space was already initiated with the end of segregation and the Group Areas Act. After 1994, land reform and land restitution started to address the consequences of apartheid's stringent control of space. The institutional transformation affected not only the political realm but also the economic sector and civil society in order to eliminate any form of discriminatory practices based on race, ethnicity or gender. Finally, personal experiences and available opportunities transformed social interactions and influenced personal feelings of well-being (Pieterse and Meintjies 2004:5–7).

Expectations, concerns and fears with respect to the individual and collective consequences of the transition varied considerably between and within the different population groups. Friedman argues that for the majority of South Africans discriminated and oppressed by apartheid, democratisation was fundamentally linked to redress, redistribution and opportunities but less to opening spaces of self-expression and choices (Friedman 2004:247).

The Challenge of Inequality and the Limitations of Change

Redistribution, poverty alleviation and infrastructural development were high on the government agenda after the first democratic elections, and there were remarkable achievements for example in access to clean water, housing and electrification (Lodge 2002:57–58). Already during the transition, the African National Congress (ANC), its alliance partners – the South African Communist Party (SACP) and the Congress of South African Trade Unions (COSATU), and a number of civil society organisations drafted a comprehensive socio-economic development strategy to confront the legacies of the past. The Redistribution and Development Programme (RDP) emphasised the critical role of the state in development and became the election manifesto of the tri-partite alliance (ANC, SACP and COSATU) for the 1994 elections. Expectations from disadvantaged population groups were high because the democratic transition and the first democratic elections brought their heroes and leaders into government. These leaders were now in a position to initiate and sustain comprehensive change, as reflected in the election campaign slogan promising "a better life for all".

Within a relatively short time, the ANC transformed itself from a liberation movement to the majority political party in government with little capacity left to review its organisational and institutional structures. The ANC's hierarchical organisational culture was at least partly a consequence of the context in which the movement operated during the liberation struggle. It was necessary for an organisation that worked illegally in South Africa to maintain strictly controlled organisational arrangements due to the hostile and dangerous environment and incidences of successful apartheid agent infiltration (Beinart 1994:212). Because of the nature and duration of the political struggle, the imprisonment of members and the urgency to continue the struggle from outside the country, the ANC consisted of broadly three different strands at the beginning of the negotiations: the iconic leadership that was imprisoned on Robben Island, the leadership in exile and the freedom fighters in the country. Suttner argues that the three strands not only differed in terms of their internal development, their liberation struggle strategies and their vision of a new South Africa, but also in terms of skills, organisational culture, political experience and maturity. Moreover, the clandestine ways in which the illegal organisation worked had consequences on internal dynamics and institutional culture. Secrecy was mutually exclusive of transparency and accountability. Personal relationships with trustworthy colleagues were critical for the survival of the movement and the individual freedom fighter (Suttner 2006:6–7).

On 10 May 1994, Nelson Mandela was sworn in as president. Soon afterwards, amidst the population's high expectations, the newly elected government realised that they inherited nearly empty state coffers. During the last months of apartheid, the old government increased the salaries, pensions and redundancy payments of officials and military personnel to ensure the allegiance of their constituency (Bell and Ntsebeza 2001:236). Foreign exchange reserves were down to less than three weeks of imports, and the budget deficit was a massive 8.6 per cent of the gross domestic product. Hence, at the time when people expected the new government to start with economic transformation and redistribution, the stabilisation of the economy was imperative to prevent capital flight. Simultaneously, South Africa's economy had to be reintegrated into an expanding, globalised marketplace. The structural shift from a mining and agricultural based economy to a manufacturing and export based economy, the dwindling gold resources, the falling gold price and the end of agricultural subsidies affected the labour market to the detriment of the huge number of unskilled workers (Sparks 2003:16–20). The extent of inequality was a challenge.

In 1996, the percentage of the total population of each population group was:

African	White	Coloured	Indian
76.5%	12.5%	8.6%	2.6%

Also in 1996, the share of income by population group was:

African	White	Coloured	Indian
35.5%	51.9%	7.9%	4.5%

(cited in Terreblanche 2002:381, 392)

Inequality was not only manifested in terms of income distribution but also in terms of uneven infrastructural development, access to healthcare, distribution of entrepreneurial, educational and economic opportunities and distribution of political, economic, military and ideological power (Terreblanche 2002:25). Moreover, the transformation and rein-tegration of the former Bantustan administrations caused additional problems. The new government depended critically on the compliance and cooperation of a demoralised state administration to implement new policies (Lodge 2002:19). Promises made during the election campaign were compromised by the realities the new government was facing (Adam et al. 1997:160).

Nevertheless, barely two years after the first democratic elections in June 1996, a new macro-economic strategy was drafted behind closed doors. It was drafted without any prior consultations and excluded the ANC's alliance partners, namely the South African Communist Party (SACP), the Congress of South African Trade Unions (COSATU) and other affiliates. The Growth, Employment and Redistribution (GEAR) strategy fo-cused on the acceleration of economic growth and was presented as a non-negotiable programme. For social organisations with a more radical vision of transformation, GEAR was a move in the wrong direction (Marais 2001:162). Terreblanche argues that the shift from RDP to GEAR was a huge mistake because it compromised the role of the state in development. As a result, the corporate sector co-opted the government as a junior partner into an economic programme that implemented a liberal capitalist version of democratic capitalism. In this programme, the role of the sovereign democratic state was severely restricted, and the enormous task of solving the legacies of apartheid and reor-ganising the economy was entrusted to free market mechanisms, with the result of serious market failures and power and income inequalities (Terreblanche 2002:446).

The secret, top-down drafting process of GEAR was criticised as incompatible with democratic practices by the different alliance partners and by individuals. According to Suttner, it affected the quality of relations within the tri-partite alliance and indicated a shift where the SACP and COSATU were less respected as equal partners but increasingly deemed "trouble makers" by the ANC leadership (Suttner 2006:21). Terreblanche's critique is even more outspoken. He states that the "distributional coalition" between the white elite and the new black elite has shaped the rearrangement of political and economic power relations after 1994 to the detriment of poor white, poor black and the poorest black households. Without significant interventions, structural inequalities perpetuate income distribution (Terreblanche 2002:38–39). Hence, GEAR was merely successful with respect to macroeconomic stabilisation while unemployment, the unequal distribution of income and poverty all increased. Economic growth is disappointing; in addition, an investment friendly environment also critically depends on sound socio-economic fundamentals (Terreblanche 2002:120–121).

Friedman argues that the alienation between the different population groups is perpetuated by the strategies that inform development and poverty alleviation programmes and the politicisation of race. Friedman emphasises that poverty reduction is not a technical matter. To effectively address the problem of inequality, poor and disadvantaged people need support from other socio-economic strata. Hence, social policy either needs the backing of significant civil society organisations, for example the trade unions, or needs to create a consensus that is justified by widely accepted criteria. According to Friedman, current poverty alleviation programmes separate the poor from the rest of society. As a result, they create the impression that the interests and needs of the poor are in conflict with the rest of society, thus marginalising the weakest groups. Social distance and the lacking consensus between the different social and political structures inhibit effective strategies to address the legacies of the past because they prevent alliances between the poor and more influential population groups (Friedman 2004:254).

The Problem of Race

Race affects social life in various ways. During apartheid, political power and citizenship rights depended on whiteness and offered material advantages (MacDonald 2006:59). Racial discrimination produced enormous inequalities and affected the distribution of opportunities and constraints. Furthermore, Erasmus emphasises how the construction of inferiority based on race influenced perceptions of self-worth among the discriminated and disadvantaged population groups (Erasmus 2005:10). The past still influences social attitudes and relations, affecting values, prejudices and perceptions of other population groups. Social relations are burdened by South Africa's history (Kometsi 2004:44). Society is deeply divided by the perpetuation of the spatial segregation and land conflicts, the lack of common history and the contrasting memories of the past. The diversity of cultural backgrounds and languages limits and constrains social interactions, levels of mutual understanding and communication in a socio-economic context of persistent inequalities and social fragmentation (Du Toit 2003:54–71).

According to Du Toit, the inherited structural and systemic imbalances, the memories of injustice and suffering of discriminated South Africans and the lack of social intimacy perpetuate the alienation between the various population groups; people live in parallel worlds (Du Toit 2003:104). Terreblanche states that social, cultural and psychological racism continues despite the quest for reconciliation because unquestioned economic conditions that maintain economic and racial inequalities limit the awareness and prevent the acknowledgement that discriminatory legislation undeservedly privileged and enriched whites at the expense of blacks (Terreblanche 2002:39). MacDonald argues that the transition from apartheid to democracy and the extension of democratic rights to all citizens was supplemented by the assurance of civil liberties, property rights and market oriented economic policies. The commitment to non-racialism within a liberal democratic system entrenched freedom, human rights and dignity but ignored and overlooked race. The denial of race neglected the structural imbalances inherited from the past and the role race continues to play in society and social relations (MacDonald 2006:178).

Habib states that at present race is more politicised than in 1994 after the first elections. He raises the question of whether racism is a relic of the past that still haunts social relations in the present or whether current political dynamics emphasise race. According to Habib, there is a difference between the past and the present emphasis on race. During apartheid, race was promoted by the white government, whereas today the former victims of apartheid advance race, albeit with different motives. Habib argues that the racialised character of redress strategies increased the politicisation of race since 1994 and also raised tensions between the different peoples of colour. The conceptualisation of empowering previously disadvantaged population group along class lines would be equally effective but less dangerous and divisive than racially based approaches (Habib 2003:240–247).

Erasmus claims that the imperative of overcoming racially defined privileges and burdens and the necessity for redress emphasise and politicise race. Racial categories are perpetuated. The problem is the hegemonic way in which the presence and legacy of race is negotiated. Quotas benefit only a small group because equity targets do not address structural imbalances (Erasmus 2005:19–21). Current redress strategies also changed the class structures within the black population and increased inequalities between poor blacks and black elites (Terreblanche 2002:391–392). Moreover, Erasmus states that new racial divisions are emerging and intersecting with nationality and citizenship rights.

Xenophobia is not new in South Africa, and expressions of xenophobia come from all population groups. Nevertheless, a worrying trend is that most of the violent xenophobic manifestations are perpetrated by black South Africans. This phenomenon is even less comprehensible considering that black South Africans were in the past victims of similar violence (Erasmus 2005:17–18).

Gibson and Gouws warn of the dangers emanating from perceived threats caused by inequality, poverty, racial animosities and crime. Political intolerance is linked to distributive grievances (Gibson and Gouws 2003:216–220). Ultimately, the divisions between the various population groups as a result of socio-economic inequalities, racial discrimination, segregation and hierarchically structured social contacts limit the acknowledgement that the different racial groups cannot survive without each other (Du Toit 2003:87–88).

The Fight Against Crime and Violence

Apartheid was a generator of violence, and victims of discrimination, oppression and social dislocation were criminalised by the state. Levels of crime were high, but for the most part crime occurred in the townships and went unnoticed. Instead of controlling crime, state policies not only contributed to the problem but also meant that law enforcement agencies and the judiciary were absorbed by political challenges (Shaw 2002:1–2). State institutions such as the police committed gross human rights violations that were accepted and legitimised in the fight against dissidents. In addition, the apartheid state criminalised behaviour that is normal in democratic societies (Du Toit 2003:115). Hence, the legitimacy of the state was contested by the discriminated population, and the criminal justice system was not a deterrent from crime. On the contrary, social status increased with convictions and jail sentences. The construction of heroes and related masculine virtues such as fearlessness, bravery and power were linked to delinquency. The destruction of socialisation structures of African families through migrant work, the Group Areas Act and forced removals of communities contributed to a breakdown in the social networks that support new generations growing up. In addition, abysmal living conditions, lacking infrastructure, endemic poverty and overcrowding increased social tensions and conflict. Discrimination and the distribution of income have social implications; enormous inequalities generate social dislocations and pathologies. The complexity of problems resulted in an environment where the use of violence is socially accepted as a means of conflict resolution (Du Toit 2003:113).

High crime rates correlate with societies in transition, where continuous violence, radical value changes and power struggles increase uncertainty and where the rule of law is contested and enforcement capacity limited. During apartheid, law enforcement agencies concentrated on politically motivated transgressions. The result was low levels of law enforcement for other offences that contributed to a feeling of impunity and reinforced bad behaviour (Du Toit 2003:113). Societies in transition and a partial breakdown of law and order are conducive to the rise of organised crime, which was exacerbated in South Africa by the disintegration in Eastern Europe, the end of the civil war in Mozambique and the demobilisation of combatants, statutory and non-statutory forces in the country (Shaw 2002:63–69).

Private security was already promoted in the 1980s by the state to increase police capacity in the townships during the insurgencies. Nevertheless, the resort to private security continued and significantly increased after the first democratic elections (Shaw 2002:110). Unacceptably high crime rates are perceived as the state's incapacity to enforce the law and not as a consequence of enormous social and economic problems. The reduction of crime is simplified into a law enforcement matter. This perception strengthens the private security sector as a replacement of the ineffective state, but it undermines the state's monopoly on coercion. Moreover, there is the problem of accountability because the private sector assumes functions of the police but refuses to be accountable to the public (Shaw 104–113). The lack of trust in the capacity of the police and the resort to private security segregates wealthier people from the community (Shaw 2002:144).

The rise of crime is also linked to generational conflicts and the lack of any prospects of decent living conditions; in particular for young men, sub-cultures not only become a way of attaining social status and recognition, they also generate solidarity and strong social bonds (Steinberg 2001:3–7). There is a correlation between protest, violence and anti-social behaviour and patterns of exclusion and lacking prospects of decent living conditions, because protest, violence and anti-social behaviour are the few political resources left to the impoverished and destitute masses with nothing to lose (Dupas 2001:1–9).

Crime not only undermines public trust but also shreds social bonds, it strengthens solidarity but also increases antagonism towards specific population groups. Moreover, Shaw emphasises the strong racial dimension of crime in South Africa. Whites are presented as victims and blacks as perpetrators of crime, which impacts on social relations and levels of intolerance and enforces racial prejudices. Shaw argues that the victimisation of specific population groups distorts realities because blacks are disproportionately affected by crime and violence: most incidents of crime occur in townships (Shaw 2002:50). However, these perceptions inform responses to the crisis.

Decentralisation and Local Government Reform

Decentralisation, the devolution of power and local government reform became a central aspect of the democratisation process, because partnership between local government and civil society is supposed to enhance the transparency of political processes and popular participation is assumed to improve responsiveness to demands and institutional efficiency and accountability (Pieterse 2002:7). The White Paper on Local Government acknowledges the necessity of national frameworks and support from the different levels of government; however, it also emphasises local structures as agents of development and states that "cities, towns and rural communities are increasingly having to find within themselves ways to make their settlements more sustainable" (White Paper 1998:41).

Nevertheless, decentralisation potentially encourages fragmentation and segmentation on the local level of politics. Decentralisation shifts the focus and responsibilities away from the central state to local political structures, which is problematic in the face of challenges such as poverty alleviation or job creation that need effective and comprehensive national strategies. It is impossible to address and resolve the legacies of apartheid on the local level. Moreover, according to Heller, there also is no reason why decentralised forms of government are more democratic (Heller 2001:132). Finally, in the context of inherited spatial segregation and its consequences, decentralisation and the significance of local government are ambiguous, potentially compromise integration and hence contribute to the fragmentation of society.

In contrast to the more impersonal nature of politics at the national level, the personalised character of political interactions at the local level can encourage manipulative practices and patronage systems. According to Khosa, in the years after the first elections there were remarkable achievements in infrastructural improvements and service delivery in the areas of housing, electrification, water, sanitation and healthcare. Nevertheless, processes were also hampered by administrative problems, constraints on institutional capacity, corruption and poor quality (Khosa 2002:142–152). In addition, tax increases and cross-subsidisation from wealthier areas with high quality infrastructure to underprivileged areas with a poor development record were contested and, for example, boycotted in affluent Johannesburg neighbourhoods (Lodge 2002:87–89). There is a common perception in wealthier neighbourhoods that most of the public resources go to the townships because wealthier neighbourhoods can look after themselves. The recourse to private investment and the privatisation of public space is a strategy in wealthier neighbourhoods, also in Norwood and Orange Grove, to overcome the limitations imposed by the current distribution of public resources.

Heller emphasises that successful decentralisation processes depend critically on the capacity of the central state because decentralisation requires coordination between the different tiers of government and regulation to ensure transparency and accountability. Devolution of power in weak states works in favour of dominant local structures or individuals and creates "decentralised despotism" (Mamdani quoted in Heller) instead of opening democratic spaces and offering participatory structures (Heller 2001:138–139). Neo-liberal politics with the promotion of the private sector and state reduction contribute to fragmentations. According to Harrison, it is increasingly difficult to define boundaries of power and responsibility between the different tiers of government and between the government, local communities and the private sector (Harrison P. 2003:15–16). Finally, in the South African context, privatisation and privatised development programmes based on the initiatives of dominant local groups are attractive to the population groups that now have less access to the state due to the transition.

The Dominance of the ANC and the Relations between the Government and the People

Despite decentralisation and the introduction of participatory local political structures, the relationship between government and civil society became increasingly ambiguous. Civil society played an important role during the liberation struggle and is still capable of challenging the state. Due to the nature of the apartheid state, civil society had a representative function and was united behind the objective of liberation. The end of apartheid also brought a diversity of expressions and increased competition between different civic and community structures (Adler and Steinberg 2000:10–12). Moreover, service delivery did not live up to people's expectations. A number of new social movements emerged and contested the state outside of institutionalised political structures. The government was offended and upset by the criticism coming from its constituency because it expected loyalty and understanding for the constraints it faced in effectively initiating comprehensive socio-economic change (Mayekiso 2003:60). Consequently, the government's vision of an active and participatory civil society started to become vague and unclear. In his speech at the 50th National Conference of the ANC in December 1997, President Mandela argued that unlike elected representation, civil society organisations often lack a popular base and therefore lack legitimacy. Hence, it is questionable whether non-governmental organisations are appropriate partners in social development and transformation processes, and it is imperative to be aware of the nature of so called organs of civil society (Mandela 1997).

Constraints on development programmes, increasing social tensions, limited state capacity and the lack of efficient strategies to address social and economic problems affect all population groups, albeit in different ways. Nevertheless, the various population groups judge state performance on the basis of delivery. Disappointment and frustration as a result of unfulfilled expectations contribute to perceptions that the state does not work among all population groups. This perception has consequences in the South African context where the various population groups have to reassess and build their relations with the state. For victims of apartheid and their conflictual experiences with the state, it is a process of building trust in the state. In contrast, for beneficiaries of apartheid who have lost confidence in the state due to the transition, it is a process of regaining confidence in the new government.

Race determines electoral affiliation (Friedman 2004:236). Despite dissatisfaction and the rise of new social movements, the overwhelming support for the ruling party contributes to particular political dynamics, because the outcome of votes is taken for granted. The political will to engage constructively with participatory structures is lacking and the suspicion of conspiring forces is increasing. There is a growing tendency to discourage electoral competition and endorse more centralised decision making structures also within the ruling party, for example the appointments of provincial and mayoral candidates by the national ANC leadership instead of their election by provincial and local branches (Friedman 2004:237–239). Moreover, as Friedman argues, the centralised approach to development and the reduced dialogue between the government and the population contributed to the limited success of reform programmes. Instead of strengthening democratic institutions, the government became more insulated. It substituted inclusion, participation and deliberation with centralisation and control. This approach to development resulted in questionable political choices, rising social tensions, the politicisation of race and the alienation of the different population groups (Friedman 2004:257).

Civil society operates within an institutional context that is defined by the state, and the quality of social resources is dependent on the broader social, political and economic environment (Harriss 2002:120). Levi argues that trust in government is a critical component of social attitudes and political interactions. Trust depends on the credibility of the government as an impartial, responsive, transparent and effective institution (Levi 1996:49). There is a historical legacy of corruption in South Africa; the apartheid regime was based on patronage and favouritism with high levels of secrecy around covert operations in order to maintain control. The oppressive nature of the state increased the powerlessness of ordinary citizens, and hence there was less popular pressure and reduced mechanisms of transparency and accountability (Lodge 1998:164, 171). After

1994, the government tried to curb corruption. However, disloyalty and demoralisation in the public sector, affirmative action, kinship loyalties in non-meritocratic appointment procedures and the creation of accountable municipalities after the reintegration of the Bantustans pose challenges. At the local level, the new political elite often lacks experience for which they compensate with social distance, lack of accountability and arrogance (Meintjies 2003:310). Certain government institutions and ministries are prone to corruption. As different interview partners of this study pointed out, corruption is a huge problem and includes the Police, Social Welfare and Home Affairs. Further notoriously corrupt practices involve the allocation of housing, government tenders and liquor licences.

Despite the commitment to combat corruption and the establishment of institutionalised control mechanisms, such as the Committee on Public Accounts, the independence of investigations into fraudulent practices is often compromised. For example government officials try to prevent the disclosure of corrupt procedures, or senior politicians launch verbal attacks on anti-corruption agencies (Lodge 2002:144–146). According to Meintjies, powerful figures publicly expressed their anger at being called to account or refused performance reviews of key programmes (Meintjies 2003:308–310). Even if unauthorised expenditures, kickbacks, irregularities in employment practices or questionable allocations of tenders are investigated, often there are no legal consequences and little is done to address maladministration (Adam et al. 1997:177). Personal relations and social networks are a critical component of corrupt practice. The problem is exacerbated by denial and lacking political will to address malpractice. Impunity for corrupt practices and behaviour creates the impression that the political elite is above the law (Mangcu 2008:96, Meintjies 310–311). Nevertheless, the behaviour of political office holders sets normative standards. It influences not only interactions between politicians and the population but also sets examples for interpersonal relations. Moreover, the lifestyle and conspicuous consumption displayed by members of the political elite are in stark contrast to the rhetoric of redistribution and erode the credibility of politicians.

The willingness of the citizenry to comply with obligations and responsibilities critically depends on the perception of the state's legitimacy and on the confidence that fellow citizens honour their obligations. The quality of politics generates political trust, and institutions provide normative standards and values that are reliable in the anonymous social environment of the modern state (Offe 1999:62–65). An institutionalised system of checks and balances has to provide structures that ensure accountability and transparency and it must allow the examination of the trustworthiness and integrity of a person in a position of political representation (Offe 1999:55–57). Perceptions of the fairness and impartiality of the state and normative standards that inform political processes influence social attitudes of citizens (Rothstein and Stolle 2003:192–200). High levels of impunity increase the volatility of the societal environment and encourage a resort to personal resources.

There are fundamental institutional preconditions that provide conditions for vibrant social life, such as political and civil rights and law and order. Social organisations have an important representative function and facilitate information flows, contact and interactions between different social structures, civil society and government. However, civil societies are divided into a variety of social institutions. There are well-connected citizens with a range of social resources, different levels of civic engagement and relative influence and power. On the other hand, there are also groups that are connected to networks that only have a limited impact on public life (Hall 2002:52–56). According to Friedman, the state has the legitimate authority to intervene if segments of civil society become destructive, but the state also has an obligation to pay attention to the diversity of interests and demands of civil society (Friedman 2004:253).

In sum, democratic consolidation in South Africa is challenged by the legacies of the past, in particular the enormous inequalities; social relations are burdened by South Africa's history (Kometsi 2004:44). Development programmes have been limited by the extent of inequalities and by constraints on resources and institutional capacity. These limiting factors have also contributed to a growing gap between popular expectations and government performance. The overwhelming support for the ANC contributes to a particular political dynamic that is reflected in lacking political will to engage with participatory structures, to reflect on criticism, to investigate malpractice and corruption or to honour requirements of accountability and transparency. This situation increases the distance between politicians and the population and reduces trust in governmental and institutional capacity and in the integrity of political elites.

3 Urban Neighbourhoods and Challenges of Cooperation and Order

The urban environment and people's perceptions of public space critically shape neighbourhoods and social life. In contrast to rural areas with dispersed settlement patterns, the population concentration in cities provides a stimulating environment for social interactions. However, spatial proximity and co-presence do not indicate the density and quality of social ties (Amin and Graham 1999). Neighbourhood relations are important facilitators of contact for interest aggregation and mobilisation. In contrast to political structures, where local government units are designated geographical entities, most social networks and organisations are not spatially defined. Nevertheless, neighbourhood sociability is critical in providing structures for social and local political engagement.

From the early beginnings of Johannesburg, access to public spaces was controlled and regulated. Even today, the past influences perceptions of order and normative aspects of sociability. The abolition of the Group Areas Act and the end of restrictions on movement changed the ways public spaces are used and increased the influx and heterogeneity of the population in formerly white neighbourhoods, an aspect of the transition that is beyond control. This chapter discusses the development of Johannesburg, and it introduces the two neighbourhoods of Norwood and Orange Grove and their shared history. After 1994, local government reform and participatory political structures in community development became a central aspect of the democratisation process. Nevertheless, it is in a context where inequalities as a result of discrimination and oppression and the effects of segregation still influence social interactions. In a social environment with uneven levels of power, unequal access to resources and population groups that have conflicting expectations and development priorities, it is debatable whether political restructuring creates genuine space for an active citizenry. Moreover, it is questionable how far social groups shape social processes and interactions, determine development objectives, influence conflict management and promote integration in a context where social interactions are burdened by the past and affected by perceptions of order and safety.

Welcome to Johannesburg – City of Gold

The discovery of gold on a Witwatersrand farm in March 1886 by George Harrison, an Australian prospector, marked the beginning of Johannesburg. In 1886, the Transvaal

Republic government's subsequent demarcation and proclamation of public diggings on a cluster of farms along the Main Reef resulted in a gold rush of exceptional proportions. Johannesburg's existence and development is intrinsically linked to the exploitation of gold and the expansion of the mining industry (Beavon 2004:20–24). To accommodate the number of prospectors, the first mining village offered 600 stands of government land to interested diggers. For a mining camp, the most suitable pattern to lay out the stands was adopted, the so-called "stand-township". It consisted of relatively small stands, with no land for market gardening or horse fodder, to allow for the accommodation of more stands (Leyds 1964:141–142). Johannes Joubert, the Surveyor General and Vice President of the Transvaal Republic, and Johannes Rissik, the stand-in for the Surveyor General responsible for the demarcations of the stands, possibly also sparked the idea for the name of the fast growing settlement. Historically, the origin of Johannesburg's name is unclear. It is certain that the city is named after a person called Johannes; however, since this name was common at the time, there are different contenders for the honour of inspiring the name of South Africa's largest city (Beavon 2004:25; Smith 1971).

At the beginning of the gold rush, a mining commissioner was in charge of the mining camp called Johannesburg, but he was already replaced by a nine member Diggers' Committee in November 1886. Nevertheless, the Diggers' Committee was inadequate for managing the expanding settlement, so five landowners – explicitly not diggers – were included in the committee. In December 1887, a Sanitary Board was elected and provided a limited form of local representation (Beavon 2004:40). Paul Kruger, the President of the Transvaal Republic, was extremely conservative in granting franchises to the growing number of foreign gold prospectors in the Witwatersrand. Incensed by Kruger's government, an influential Randlord, Leander Jameson, tried to overthrow the government in December 1895. Despite the failure of the insurgency, Kruger had to make concessions and finally converted the Sanitary Board into a municipal government in 1897 as a consequence of the Jameson Raid (Beavon 2004:32).

The limitations of early Johannesburg's administrative and political organisation become more apparent if one considers that already in 1888, the settlement had a population of between 8000 and 9000 people. The number of people arriving on the Witwatersrand triggered the development of a service infrastructure including estate agents, banks, lawyers, businesses, health facilities and entertainment locales. The first newspaper, *The Star*, started publishing in 1887. In 1891, a system of public transport was initiated: the horse-drawn tram. Stuttaford's, a three storey department store, opened in 1892. Hotels were important for the many new arrivals. In addition, prostitution thrived due to the gender division of work, the nature of the mining industry and the beginning of migrant work

(Beavon 2004:52–57). In 1889, a farm called Lemoen Plaas (Orange Grove in English) that was situated along the road from Johannesburg to Pretoria advertised land available on lease for a hotel. The Orange Grove Hotel was not only a convenient stop-over on a trip to Pretoria. Its beautiful tea garden was also popular for its Sunday afternoon concerts and as a recreational area in the countryside; as a result, it attracted residents from the nearby City of Johannesburg (Smith 1971:383).

The expanding mining sector had little control over the cost of imported equipment for deep level mining; hence, exploitative labour conditions were the most feasible option for keeping production costs low. Land grabs and taxation forced the indigenous population into wage employment with no bargaining leverage as unskilled labourers. To control the influx into Johannesburg, pass legislation was adopted in 1896. Additional restrictions limited freedom of movement and association for indigenous workers. The growing mining industry's demand for cheap labour resulted in the recruitment of migrant workers from rural areas in Southern Africa. This migration had detrimental social consequences for African families and their socialisation structures. In contrast, white mine workers had better salaries and less dangerous working conditions since they usually supervised African miners and were in a superior position within the mines' social hierarchy. Moreover, the poorly paid African mine workers were encouraged to spend their meagre salaries in the bars around the mining camps, often resulting in a vicious circle of debt and forced labour. Mine workers were not allowed to bring their families and were usually entitled to only one annual home leave, which had an impact on family structures, paternal responsibilities and child care. The hard and unhealthy working conditions affected the health of mine workers in a context with no healthcare entitlements or social security. Once miners were unfit to continue with the hard work in the mines, they were forced to return home and became the responsibility of their families. In addition, employers had no obligation to give compensation in cases of injury or death resulting from dangerous working conditions (Beavon 2004: 32–36).

Apart from facing restrictions of movement and controlled access to the city, non-white workers also had to live in designated areas. As early as 1900, government measures to control health hazards and honour commitments to public health standards resulted in the first forced relocation of the Malay population and the subsequent destruction of the Coolie Location (Beavon 2004:75). Further legislation, in particular the Native Land Act of 1913 and the Natives Urban Areas Act of 1923, limited access to land and housing for the non-white population to Native Reserves and three freehold areas where Africans could acquire property: Alexandra, Sophiatown and Kliptown (Beavon 204:95, Davenport 1991:1–5). Unlike other cities, Johannesburg was not founded on a site with access to water or along an attractive trade route; rather, it was founded for its promising development potential and prospects of wealth (Murray 2008:1). As a consequence, segregation, discriminatory legislation, exploitative labour conditions and the control of public space were consciously devised and implemented. They are intrinsically linked to the expansion of the mining industry and the rise of capitalism. Hence, urban space was not only demarcated, divided and allocated; it was also a central foundation of the political and social order (Robinson 1998:533).

In 1899, the start of the Boer War between the British Empire and the two independent Boer Republics, the Orange Free State and the Transvaal Republic, prompted an exodus from Johannesburg; nevertheless, the interruption of gold production was short. Seven months later in May 1900, British forces occupied and secured Johannesburg and Pretoria, mining resumed and Johannesburg continued to prosper and grow (Beavon 2004:67–71). In 1896, ten years after the discovery of gold in the Witwatersrand, Johannesburg's population was already approximately 73,500. In 1911 it was 240,000. In 1936, at fifty years old, Johannesburg's population exceeded half a million (Beavon 2004:83). The city continued to spread around the central business district into new townships and suburbs, expanding its infrastructure and services sectors accordingly.

Norwood and Orange Grove

In 1902, Alexander Osborne, Dr. Cecil Schultz and J.T. Grant, the owners of the freehold township called Norwood, announced stands 25 minutes away from Market Square. The stands were along "a magnificent road to be made" and "Norwood is the coming Suburb". The three owners of the township named the streets after their spouses and children. Dr. Schultz changed his German-sounding name to Scholtz, and since he did not have a family, he named streets after his mother, sisters and friends. Wolfgang Road is named after Scholtz's gardener, a former run-away sailor (Smith 1971:372, 488, 588). An area called Alexandria Estate or Alexandra in 1904, was already known for the Orange Grove Hotel and Tea Garden. The area was taken over by the African Realty Trust. The layout was changed, and on 1 April 1904, stands were advertised in the township that was now called Orange Grove after the hotel. "A veritable paradise where the air was salubrious and free from the polluted atmosphere of the town" (Smith 1971:383–384, Godfrey 1974). The African Reality Trust, a company dealing with real estate and mining concessions in the "Transvaal Colony or elsewhere in Africa" and founded by the American entrepreneur Isidore Schlesinger, used numbered streets and avenues to demarcate the locations of the stands (Sharieff et al. 2007:315). Infrastructural development also brought electrification, piped water, sewerage and street lights to the two neighbourhoods. In 1911 the electric tram started to serve the area (Beavon 2004:90–91, Bruce 1983:27–31).

The stands for property development in Norwood and Orange Grove were rather small, ranging from 15m by 30m to 30m by 30m, so relatively densely populated neighbourhoods resulted (Beavon 2004:89, Bruce 1983:31, Smith 1971:372, 384). However, the two neighbourhoods differ significantly in size since Norwood is less than half the spatial extension of Orange Grove. Grant Avenue and Louis Botha Avenue contributed to the commercial development of the two neighbourhoods with shops and businesses. According to an article in *The Star* newspaper, the "typical village atmosphere", particularly in Norwood, provided a sense of cohesion and identity that encouraged neighbourly relations between residents (anonymous, The Star, 1986). Norwood Primary School and Orange Grove Primary School improved the infrastructure of the two neighbourhoods and added to their attractiveness for families with children. In neighbourhoods with a diversity of functional uses including living, shopping, offices, schools and leisure, the number of people in the streets provide a degree of security and social control (Jacobs 1961:245).

The development of the two neighbourhoods is interconnected despite the fact that Orange Grove is much larger than Norwood. The small segment of Orange Grove west of Louis Botha Avenue is nearly the size of Norwood and home to the Orange Grove West Residents' Organisation. Orange Grove had a significant Italian immigrant population. The African Explosives and Chemicals Industries in Modderfontein opened at the end of the 19th century, supplying the growing gold industry with explosives for underground mining and the agricultural sector with fertilisers. The industry depended on the expertise of foreign immigrants. In Italy during World War I, women were trained to pack dynamite into waxed paper for the military. After the end of the war, the skills of these Italian women were useful in South Africa, and a considerable number were employed by the African Explosives and Chemicals Industries in Modderfontein. Orange Grove was the closest residential area. Hence, the Italian factory workers looked for properties in Orange Grove, significantly shaping the community and the specific characteristics of "Little Italy" (Usher 1973). In contrast, Norwood attracted white middle class residents and predominantly English speakers.

Until the 1980s, the two neighbourhoods had only a small number of black residents: domestic staff living on their employer's property or workers employed by the shops or business sector in the vicinity. For the non-white population, already restricted choices regarding residential options and movement in the city were even more limited with the rise of apartheid after the 1948 elections. The Group Areas Act and pass laws controlled and restrained the movement of Africans, monitoring access to white residential areas. Employers were in a powerful position to manage, monitor and control admittance into residential neighbourhoods. The right of entry into white residential areas and the movement of African workers depended on the consent of their employers; moreover, social relations and interactions between white residents and the African population occurred in a context of strictly institutionalised and internalised social hierarchies.

Nevertheless, a complete implementation of the Group Areas Act was never achieved. The relocation of Africans living in residential areas assigned to the white population, for example Alexandra Township, was impossible to enforce due to mounting resistance. In addition, a complete control of the influx of illegal non-white residents into the cities was not feasible and unworkable. After the Soweto uprising in 1976, a growing number of white South Africans understood the cost of the unviable political system. Moreover, the housing and transport crises exacerbated in the 1980s, further reducing the apartheid government's ability to manage the influx of the non-white population. The government had to make concessions, so the "greying" of demarcated white residential areas in Johannesburg was an attempt to control an increasingly uncontrollable development. The Group Areas Act was further undermined by the business sector because employers made their residential properties in the city available to their employees. Many advantages such as avoiding transport problems and long travel times were additional incentives to accommodate non-white employees in the city (Beavon 2004:214–217). Apartheid laws also regulated matrimony but only prohibited marriages between whites and non-whites; marriages between the different non-white population groups were allowed. In 1985, the repeal of the inter-marriage prohibitions further obstructed the enforcement of the Group Areas Act because inter-marriages between different racial groups rendered the allocation of designated residential areas according to race unmanageable (Cloete 1991:92–93).

In 1983, the Norwood and Orchards Residents' Association (NORA) opposed a planned compound that Johannesburg's Cleaning Department wanted to construct for their workers in the neighbourhood, and NORA prepared for a hearing with the municipality's management committee. Their principal objection was that a hostel block would be an eye sore in the appearance of the suburb (anonymous, Eastern Tribune 1983). Five years later in 1988, the "Five Freedoms Forum" conducted a survey in Norwood on white attitudes with respect to the Groups Areas Act. 70 per cent of the participants were in favour of its abolition, and 57 per cent of this group in favour of abolition were convinced that the changes would not cause any problems. Nevertheless, 68 per cent of the entire sample regarded the following problems likely to emanate from the abolition of the Group Areas Act: overcrowding, development of slums, increase of noise, rowdiness and lower neighbourhood standards (anonymous, FFF 1988).

The greying of the inner city and Hillbrow was facilitated by economic factors. The growing wealth of the white population allowed the move from flats to properties in the suburbs, boosting the availability of flats in town. The option of asking much more rent from non-white, illegal residents was an incentive to favour non-white tenants, which increased the number of non-white residents in the inner city and Hillbrow. Nonetheless, the reputation of these neighbourhoods declined, negatively impacting on property values and making property owners reluctant to invest in the maintenance of their buildings. The deterioration of buildings together with overcrowding due to housing shortages contributed to uneasiness and prejudices of the white population against the non-white population moving into their neighbourhood (Beavon 2004:126–220). This development encouraged the remaining white population to leave their inner city residences and Hillbrow. Norwood and Orange Grove were indirectly affected by the greying of Hillbrow and later Berea and Yeoville because the Jewish population from these neighbourhoods started to relocate to Norwood and Orange Grove (interview Jewish community 2007). The abolition of the Group Areas Act in 1991 put an official end to an already dysfunctional and completely undermined legislation. Still, perceptions and prejudices of deteriorating standards in formerly white neighbourhoods due to the influx of non-white people persist, and white residents tend to relocate as soon as the number of non-white

Fig. 1: Radium Beer Hall

Fig. 2: Louis Botha Avenue

residents exceeds a certain threshold. In Orange Grove, the declining value of properties close to Louis Botha Avenue attracts non-white buyers. The number of relocating white residents from this neighbourhood increases the number of available properties. The supply exceeds the demand for houses and contributes to the decreasing value of these properties. According to different interview partners, this area is a concern for the residents' association and the ward committee because it affects the reputation of the entire neighbourhood; the Orange Grove City Improvement District project is a response to this development.

During the years of segregation, one of the few racially integrated locations and the first multi-racial bar in town was the Radium Beer Hall in Orange Grove. Established in 1929 as the Radium Tea Hall, the owner sold more alcoholic beverages illegally than tea. His customers included black workers in the area, who were not allowed to drink. In 1944, the owner acquired a wine and malt licence and changed the name to Radium Beer Hall. It became the "biggest shebeen in town" (Pendock 1999, Unsworth 2000). The Radium Beer Hall with its Jazz performances was one of the few places in the two neighbourhoods, except for private homes and churches, where different racial groups could interact despite the stringent apartheid legislation.

The two commercial areas around Grant Avenue and Louis Botha Avenue influenced the development of Norwood and Orange Grove. Grant Avenue has different shops, restaurants and service providers. Louis Botha Avenue is the main transit corridor between

Fig. 3: Shop Louis Botha Avenue

Alexandra Township and the inner city of Johannesburg. Grant Avenue and Louis Botha Avenue are less than one kilometre apart from each other; nevertheless, in recent years Louis Botha Avenue has started to deteriorate which affects both neighbourhoods. Once a sprawling commercial area, Louis Botha Avenue is today at the centre of the Orange Grove City Improvement District. Many shops and service providers moved away and were replaced by second hand, pawn, a few grocery and fast food shops. In addition, there are a number of Nigerian owned cellphone shops or video rental shops for Nollywood movies with illegal bars in the back of the buildings.

There are also a considerable but changing number of Pentecostal Churches along Louis Botha Avenue, two traditional healers have a shop on Louis Botha Avenue, and there is a bead wholesale store. The bars are an on-going problem. Apparently, many are operating illegally. Residents complain because the music is loud, drunk people shout and fight in the street – which is irritating particularly after midnight – and there is the problem of prostitution. During the day, pedestrians along Louis Botha Avenue are mostly Africans with only very few exceptions.

A few businesses have survived in the changing environment, among them the Radium Beer Hall and Supersconto, an Italian supermarket located on the third floor of the Standard Bank building. Both enterprises attract customers from all over town, and Supersconto provides parking facilities. Property owners are reluctant to invest in the infrastructure of their properties, and in the vicinity of Louis Botha, property values are declining. However, there is a residential development and redevelopment planned between Davidson Street and Hathorn Avenue. According to the Regional Spatial Development Framework's functional road classification, Louis Botha is a mobility spine prioritising traffic flow (Johannesburg City Council 2004).

In contrast, Grant Avenue is classified as an activity street by the Regional Spatial Development Framework (Johannesburg City Council 2004). Mobility is compromised in favour of activity, meaning for example space for pedestrians or street cafés. Grant Avenue still attracts the middle class; however, smaller shops are battling to survive, there are a few empty shops and a number of properties need renovation.

A critical focus of the business and residents' associations is the conservation of Grant Avenue. Unfortunately, it was not possible to get the support of more than 51% of the shops and property owners, the critical mass, in order to promote a collective improvement effort. So far investment into the conversion of Grant Avenue as an activity street has not yet materialised.

Despite the short distance to Grant Avenue, residents nowadays use their cars to go to the shops. The changing attitudes towards public space and fear of crime cause many residents to use their cars even for a short distance; hence parking is a problem in the vicinity of Grant Avenue. Today, there are fairly big parking facilities in front of Woolworths and Spar, the two supermarkets at the corner of Grant Avenue and William Road. However, to get to the shops along Grant Avenue, customers rarely find parking in Grant Avenue

Fig. 4: Grant Avenue

and have to park further away and walk. An increasing number of residents considers it more convenient to go to shopping malls, not only because of the parking facilities but also because of the concentration of shops in the same location. The development of the Norwood Pick n Pay Hypermarket into a full shopping mall less than two kilometres away is a potential threat to business along Grant Avenue.

In 2005, the construction of a mall was prevented in Paterson Park just behind Grant Avenue. The City Council intended to sell a portion of Paterson Park to developers arguing that the park has become home to homeless people and what local residents call "vagrants", so local residents refrain from using it. NORA, the Orange Grove Residents' Associations and the business sector along Grant Avenue vehemently opposed the project. They not only wanted to retain the recreational area, there were also concerns that the development would compromise their efforts to revitalise Grant Avenue. In addition, open public space in the area is already limited, and the development would reduce the available space even more. Finally, according to residents Norwood is a village type neighbourhood and not the location for a shopping mall. Today, a small townhouse development is planned in the north corner of Paterson Park, and the rest remains recreational space.

In contrast, the development of the Houghton Golf course, a recreational space at the fringe of Norwood was supported and promoted by members of NORA and the Orange Grove Residents' Associations. Residents around the Golf Course vehemently opposed the project and were upset about the lacking information and consultation with them.

Fig. 5: Coffee Shop Grant Avenue

Fig. 6: Shopping Area Spar and Woolworth

They bitterly complained about the intransparent way this matter was handled by the different residents' organisations and ward committees that were supposed and claimed to represent them.

The Paterson Park Recreation Centre is located between Orange Grove and Norwood. It was constructed at the beginning of the 1960s with the intention of providing community and social infrastructure to the population. According to the Regional Manager of Sports, Recreation and Aquatics, the economic boom after World War II, structural changes in the economy, shorter working hours of household heads and the increasing number of household appliances making life easier for housewives resulted in more leisure time for middle class families. The reduction in working hours and household chores contributed to a different time management. The government was concerned with the quality of leisure activities and entertainment of the white population. The construction of community centres was a contribution to the provision of space for suitable and proper leisure activities. The Paterson Park Recreation Centre has different rooms, a hall with a stage and a separate assembly hall. Outdoor facilities offer sports fields, tennis courts and a park. The centre is located behind the Norwood Police Station. Paterson Park itself extends across the Police Station and 9th Street. A much larger portion of Paterson Park is north of 9th Street, and there was a public swimming pool in that section of the park. Unfortunately, during the different stages of Johannesburg's municipal restructuring, responsibilities regarding pool maintenance were unclear and neglected to such an

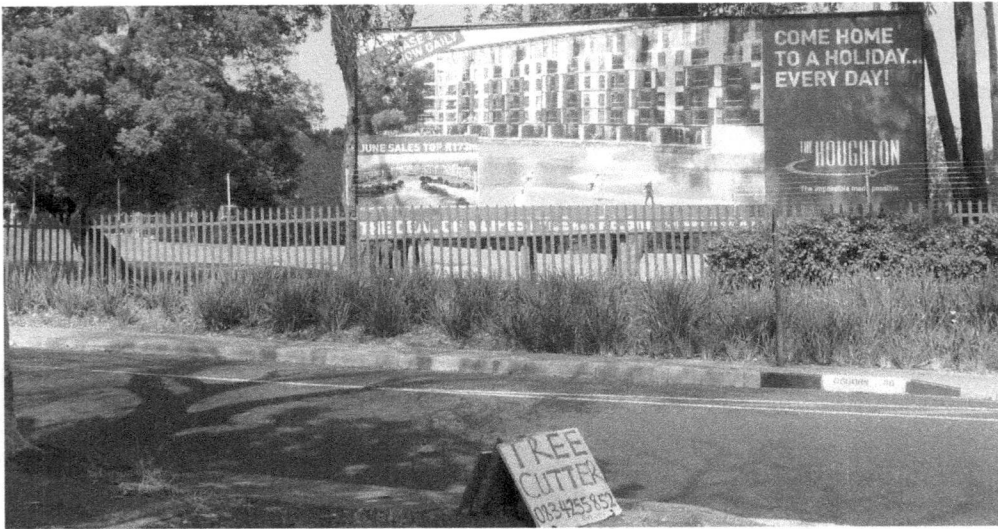

Fig. 7: Houghton Residential Development

extent that today the pool is beyond repair. Paterson Park and the Recreation Centre are the focus of a major community development project intending to facilitate better community interactions.

The police barracks are behind the Norwood Police Station bordering the Paterson Park Recreation Centre. This huge block of flats is accommodation for the more than 150 police force members working at the station and their families. The barracks are overcrowded and in dire need of renovation. The area around the buildings is disintegrating: there are heaps of garbage in the back yard, and the outside area is badly maintained. A large number of children live in the barracks and, according to the Councillors and residents' associations, many are not supervised during the day. The barracks have a bad reputation. The changing racial composition of the police force resulted in a considerable influx of African families into the area. Due to the number of people living in the barracks, they have changed the racial composition and levels of homogeneity in the neighbourhood.

Democratisation and Local Government Reform

During apartheid until 1991, Johannesburg was divided into thirteen local government entities that differed in terms of their resource base, service infrastructure and opportunities. They fell under different legal and planning systems (Beall et al. 2002:74). Before

1995, the Johannesburg City Council spent on average R3000 annually per resident of the northern suburbs, but only R500 annually per resident of Soweto (Lodge 2002:86). Different transitional metropolitan governmental structures planned and coordinated the transition and transformation of local institutions between 1991 to 1995. They initiated the local government reform process in order to address and reverse the spatial legacies and inequalities of apartheid (Beall 2002:74). Today, Johannesburg is divided into seven different regions that are subdivided into local wards, the most decentralised political unit. Norwood and Orange Grove are in two different local government wards, but both wards belong to Region E of the City of Johannesburg Municipality. Decentralisation and participatory local government structures were critical strategies of the democratisation process that took place in a challenging context due to the complexity of inequalities in Johannesburg.

Robinson argues that due to the power sharing agreement of the Government of National Unity, it was possible for the representation of powerful interests to dominate the design of local government structures and to ensure a veto right for minorities in key local decision-making processes (Robinson 1997:366; 1998:381). The preservation of the particular character of certain urban neighbourhoods was viewed as a desirable aspect of decentralisation and the accommodation of diversity. Subsequently, specific zoning and planning norms were devised to protect privileges in wealthy neighbourhoods. Proposals even included a second ballot for property owners in local elections

Fig. 8: Police Barracks

(Robinson 1998:537). The manipulation of the devolution process and its undemocratic demands perpetuated the segregated residential environments, politicising and racialising local boundaries (Robinson 1997:366). Local demarcations have a critical impact on the weight of votes by the different racial groups and hence are linked to political choices (Robinson 1998:542–543). Despite the end of apartheid and segregation, discrimination continues not as a result of biased legislation but in terms of geographical and socio-economic location (Shapiro 2002:111).

During apartheid, residents' organisations in Norwood and Orange Grove were main-ly concerned with service provision, infrastructural development and maintenance. How-

Figs. 9 and 10: Paterson Park Recreation Centre

ever, the situation differed significantly from the present because many more resources were available for white residential areas, and their allocation was less contested. For the Norwood and Orchards Residents' Association (NORA) it meant less work and a more approachable institutional context. According to NORA members, the association was never concerned with the social development of the community and the quality of social relations. Neighbours knew each other and socialised in the neighbourhood. Hence it was not necessary to organise specific events that would introduce community members to each other.

The quality of services, infrastructural development and maintenance are critical components to assess government performance in local communities (Lodge 2002:86). In post-apartheid South Africa, local political structures, the two ward councillors and residents' organisations focus on two sets of problems: firstly, they are concerned with the quality of services and the allocation of resources for infrastructural maintenance. Secondly, they concentrate on the control of urban space and law enforcement in response to illegal businesses, the expanding informal sector and the influx of the urban poor into wealthier suburbs. The failure of the urban government to address these problems not only effectively undermines the legitimacy of the municipal administration, but in an environment of perceived disorder ordinary citizens are also more reluctant to comply with rules and regulations (Murray 2008:24).

In the context of conflicting interests, the meaning of participatory structures and community driven development is contested because the nature of the community critically depends on the question of inclusion and exclusion (Biggs 1997:115). Furthermore, manifestations of power are often hidden in social practice. The focus on community obscures the influence of power on social dynamics and local political processes, for example in terms of priorities or acceptable behaviour (Cooke and Kothari 2001:14). During apartheid, state power and political order critically depended on spatial arrangements. There was a strong correlation between control, orderliness and law enforcement in public spaces; the apartheid geography and the organisation of urban space was a significant element that secured state capacity (Robinson 1998:365–366, 377–378). Moreover, assessments of acceptable behaviour and desirable development are shaped by socialisation processes: individual and collective experiences set normative standards that inform responses to disorder and perceived threats (Kim 2005:199). Perceptions of public order are still influenced by apartheid standards that pathologised and problematised behaviour normal in liberal societies and that was only enforceable by an authoritarian state (Du Toit 2003:115).

Attitudes to Public Space

Apartheid not only regulated, restricted and controlled access and use of public space, it also profoundly influenced the social interactions and perceptions of other population groups. In post-apartheid South Africa, access and utilisation of public space continues to be monitored by various social forces. Despite constitutional rights and the abolition of the Group Areas Act, de facto not everyone is welcome or can enjoy the same rights in neighbourhood public spaces. Access to public space is often determined by assumptions based on decency and moral worth; hence, public space is open for those who deserve it and are considered capable of acting in a responsible and predictable way (McDowell 1999:111ff). In particular, black people are scrutinised, and if they are well dressed and look employed they cause less concerns. In contrast, if black people look impoverished and "hang around", they are quickly classified as homeless. One of the NORA members argues that "vagrants" cause huge problems because they increase insecurity, often commit crime and contribute to the disintegration of the neighbourhood. Moreover, especially long-term residents are reluctant to adapt to the changing environment. Long-standing customs and norms are defended, and newcomers in the two neighbourhoods are accepted only if they respect and adjust to these standards. Conflict arises not only between different population groups but also between generations. A wide range of issues cause conflict: from order, noise levels and the way people dress to the types of businesses and the changing selection of food at the Spar supermarket adapted to a more diverse clientele.

Apartheid affected the micro-level of social interactions, and desegregation resulted in contrasting experiences for the different population groups (Durrheim 2005:456). The end of segregation has not yet resulted in the end of racial boundaries and interpersonal distance; inevitable informal or spontaneous contacts in public spaces are frequently guided by internalised and unreflected behavioural patterns. In addition, segregation and isolation fostered the development of negative stereotypes and pessimistic expectations regarding the quality of intergroup relations. Negatively perceived interracial contacts, particularly the racialised perception of crime, are damaging, increase tensions and perpetuate prejudices, specifically against impoverished non-whites.

The incapacity of the state to address inequality and poverty in a sustainable way has consequences for neighbourhood sociability and intergroup relations. The urban poor have no choice but to live in the streets and look for ways to sustain themselves. In the public eye, the structural problem arising from unemployment and poverty becomes a matter of law enforcement. Perceptions of disorder arise from informal economic activity such as hawkers or car guards and homeless people. They are seen as threats to morals, decency and sanitary conditions because they not only sleep but also wash themselves in public spaces. As a consequence, survivalist strategies are criminalised, and order is re-established by getting rid of them (Murray 2008:19–20).

There is a strong perception that homeless people and hawkers are a threat to safety and negatively impact business. NORA together with the business sector and the Councillor tried to find a permanent solution for the hawkers displaying their goods on the sidewalks and in front of Woolworths and Spar. A fixed installation with shelves for merchandise was installed for the hawkers to use and to keep them away from the shops. The installation is at the corner of Grant Avenue and Ivy Road one block away from the shopping area in front of Woolworths and Spar. The hawkers were neither asked nor included in discussions for a solution to the conflicting interests but were expected to cooperate. Instead of re-establishing their business on the sidewalks in front of Woolworth and Spar, the hawkers started to walk around with their merchandise, not only in front of the shops but also along Grant Avenue. The mobility of the hawkers renders it more difficult to chase them away. The difficulty of finding a sustainable solution is illustrated by the following example. Three homeless women originally from Zimbabwe and already staying in the area for several years, sleep and wash themselves in the park. Repeatedly this problem is discussed at Community Police Forum (CPF) meetings, and residents demanded that the police arrest them. However, the police argued that one of the women was very sick. So if they arrested the women, they would have to bring the sick woman to hospital where she would be treated at the taxpayers' expense (CPF meeting, 31 October 2007). In May 2008, the problem was raised again at a CPF meeting. Due to the cold temperatures, the women moved closer to the buildings and would sleep in house and shop entrances. One of the hairdressers on Grant Avenue was unable to access her business because of the "sleeping vagrants" in front of the door. The police was asked to arrest them. The station commissioner argued that this would be a useless exercise because they would return straight away after their release. One of the residents got increasingly agitated and yelled, "well then arrest them again and if they return, arrest them again and again until they are fed up and don't return any more. Enough is enough and something has to happen now, now" (CPF meeting 28 May 2008).

In certain areas of the two neighbourhoods, law enforcement is quasi non-existent. Most prominently, there is almost no response to the permanent problems of drug trafficking, prostitution and illegal bars along Louis Botha Avenue. It is impossible to address these offences locally without an integrated strategy and the cooperation of the city and the province. Noise levels and alcohol consumption are not only a problem along Louis Botha with its many illegal bars; two clubs in the vicinity of Grant Avenue have also

Fig. 11: Road Closure off Louis Botha

caused a lot of trouble. The clubs attract young middle class people in huge numbers, a completely different clientele to that of Louis Botha Avenue's bars. Since the residential areas start right behind Grant Avenue, residents are intimidated by the number of cars arriving and looking for parking, and the noise from laughing, shouting and music.

The limitations of law enforcement and feelings of powerlessness also influence social interactions in residential neighbourhoods and among the business sector. Residents are less interested in the neighbourhood and have withdrawn into the private sphere. According to one of the councillors people are not only indifferent, they also cannot be bothered with their responsibilities towards neighbours. This is reflected in the transgression of property boundaries, unlicensed construction, car parking on sidewalks, trees growing over walls, littering and the unwillingness to honour obligations, for example in cases of damage to common space or other properties. Businesses, especially coffee shops, construct unlicensed verandas on Grant Avenue to offer tables outside the buildings on the sidewalks. A number of property owners along Grant and especially along Louis Botha Avenue do not assume their responsibility to invest in building maintenance. The result is a vicious circle: it is not worth investing in property in disintegrating neighbourhoods, yet at the same time, the decaying infrastructure contributes to neighbourhood disintegration. The decline of personal contacts in the neighbourhood reduces levels of social control and the violation of social norms becomes less costly. The result is a sense of impunity exacerbated by weak law enforcement. Furthermore, in a context of asymmetric relations the powerful can ignore social norms and hawkers and homeless people are disproportionately victimised.

Disorder, Crime and the Privatisation of Public Space

Perceptions of order and disorder are critically linked to the problem of crime. Safety and security are legitimate concerns that influence social interactions. Crime undermines social trust and public confidence; perceptions of crime and insecurity perpetuate and reinvent social categories and stereotypes (Shaw 2002:85). In the face of disorder and loss of control, the privatisation of public space is a strategy for managing urban disorder and ensuring a sense of stability and confidence (Davis 2003:202). Insecurity contributes to the proliferation of gated communities and controlled urban spaces such as shopping malls, where right of admission is reserved in an environment of conflicting rights. These security clusters produce a form of exclusive citizenship and restrict opportunities of interactions across social divisions in the public realm. The government's incapacity to address structural inequalities and ensure stability has increased the authority of the private and corporate sectors. Especially private security is thriving. The provision of facilities outside the state enables citizens as consumers to control the quality of services. There are different road closures in Norwood, in particular to prevent access from Louis Botha Avenue and a number of private security companies operate in the area.

So far, various efforts of residents to control larger areas of public space by cooperating with private security companies have failed. Nevertheless, it is a worrying development because as soon as more than 51% per cent of citizens are in favour of access control by private security, the remaining residents in those areas are forced to participate and contribute financially towards privatised security. This undermines the state's monopoly on

Fig. 12: Gated Community

coercive institutions. Moreover, private security is not bound by requirements of transparency and accountability.

In gated communities, people constrain themselves and their social interactions. Walls produce extreme forms of insular subjectivity, normalise paranoid attitudes, demonise the other and generate chronic anxiety. They restrict opportunities for interactions reaching across social boundaries (McLaughlin and Muncie 1999:120–122).

In these insular arrangements, social relations among residents increase at the expense of more integrated social structures. In addition, in these security clusters fear is a function of security mobilisation. Fear creates its own demands that are less about safety and more about insulation and control (Davis 2003:202–203). The rhetoric of safety for law-abiding citizens and the right to security justifies spatial strategies that keep unwanted elements away and ensure class privileges. The privatisation of public space not only generates new forms of exclusion but also perpetuates patterns of spatial hierarchies, promoting an indifference to the plight of the poor (Murray 2008:25–26). The focus on individuals and groups instead of their structural interdependence results in skewed perceptions. Order and safety become a question of mentality and attitude, not of material means. Similarly, unemployment is not recognised as structural but seen as a matter of choice (Shapiro 2002:109).

The fear of crime and negative perceptions of public space encourage the use of the car instead of walking, even for short distances. Nevertheless, car users navigate in an impersonal space as human interactions are reduced to a minimum, so that possible anti-social attitudes develop (Hamilton and Hoyle 1999:79–81). The lifestyle of the middle class has evolved around the car. Even for children, personal relations, school, leisure and entertainment are not rooted in the neighbourhood, and they depend on transport (Blowers and Pain 1999:277). For unaccompanied children, the use of public space is denied; it is not only a question of transport but also a response to danger. Social activities become less spontaneous and more controlled, and children are deprived of significant social experiences (Hamilton and Hoyle 1999:75).

The superficiality of relations in the public space of neighbourhoods have an element of uncertainty and hence are neglected, a situation that is exacerbated by crime and violence. Moreover, there is a degree of helplessness in the face of problems that exceed individual agency. Neighbours do not know each other as closely as they know family and friends, and they do not socialise in the same regular way. These more superficial relations appear trivial and negligible. Nevertheless, public spaces provide the opportunity to engage with people one does not want to know closely but needs to engage with because these more instrumental interactions are relevant for neighbourhood cooperation and development.

Despite the ambiguity of public space and the reluctance of social engagement, neighbourhood sociability is a central communication structure. It enables information flows and provides space for the mediation of conflict, for development planning and for the exchange of opinions and interest articulation (Jacobs 1961:55–56). In a context of high levels of crime, the revival of the neighbourhood reverses the anonymity of public space. The chairperson of the Gauteng Province CPF coordination structure stresses that crime rates are lower in neighbourhoods where residents know each other, feel responsible for the maintenance of public space and assume ownership (interview 2008).

Towards an Integrated Community

Community development and social programmes are important features of urban planning and administration. Programmes conducted by Johannesburg's municipal authorities and different institutions shape community life, provide services and safe spaces, offer education or entertainment and contribute to stability. The legacies of apartheid and the fragmentation of society are a challenge to community development and it is debatable whether interventions and programmes of social engineering are capable of addressing alienation and social distance, facilitating integration and constructing a more inclusive identity. The municipality in Johannesburg invests considerable resources into community development, nevertheless, diversity, low levels of trust and crime all work against integration in Johannesburg's neighbourhoods. In this context, the question arises which community structures are attractive, inviting, safe and visible enough to encourage use by community members and build bridges between the different social groups. For example, the municipality invested in the infrastructure of the parks in both neighbourhoods, and special attention was paid to the playgrounds. The parks are used, but mainly by the African population or by nannies looking after white children. Parents do not have the habit of spending an afternoon together with other families on the playground.

Paterson Park Recreation Centre is a community development project for which the City of Johannesburg employs a chairperson or coordinator. There are different programmes suggested and coordinated by the municipality. The programmes are designed to encourage community development and address problems such as xenophobia, migrants and youth problems and to improve information flows. According to the Regional Manager of Sports, Recreation and Aquatics, xenophobia is a serious problem and also affects relations among South Africans. The appearance of the community centre is a problem as it does not look attractive. Furthermore, information channels are limited, the centre is not visible and the community is still very segregated making it difficult to reach out to the different population groups. For example, the migrant community is very transient and changes rapidly; it is difficult to maintain a relationship and know what they need. A development project intends to revamp the centre and make it more appealing. Currently, the access road to the centre leads through a residential area which is a source of conflict, especially on weekends. The access will be moved to 9th Street, next to the police station, and the new entrance will be situated just around the corner of Grant Avenue next to the Norwood Library, bringing it closer to the community. Grant Avenue is marked as an activity street by the City Council and eventually traffic will be reduced. The police station and the barracks will be integrated into the area development. The dilapidated swimming pool will be removed and the entire area of the park across 9th Street will be rehabilitated to make it more attractive.

The Paterson Park Recreation Centre is currently less used for informal sociability than for different structured activities and courses; actually, the course facilitators pay rent for their rooms, and the courses are listed in the centre's information booklet. The courses are open to everybody but at a fee. They range from Karate to Scrabble and from Belly Dancing to Domestic Workers' Skills Development. There are courses for children, sports clubs and self-help groups, namely Narcotics Anonymous and Stroke Aid.

The coordinator of the centre is not directly involved in the courses or activities but facilitates the rental of the rooms and interacts with the course facilitators. The City Council has decided to stop renting the facility to Pentecostal Churches because they are very exclusive, which is not in the interests of community development. Different community organisations, for example the residents' associations and the CPF, use the centre for meetings. There are kitchen facilities with dishes and cutlery. Tables and chairs are available for a fee, and the hall with the stage is popular for weddings, discos and conferences. The sports facilities are used by different clubs, and the children from the police barracks play in the park or use the sports facilities.

The two libraries in the community, the Norwood Library and the Orange Grove Reference Library, attract all population and age groups. The interest in books and reading is a common denominator that cuts across social barriers. The reference library is funded by the city, and there are no fundraisers necessary. According to the two librarians the atmosphere is very relaxed and every day a number of people just come to read because the library has a selection of daily and weekly newspapers and magazines. Some people sit in the library and read for a short while, others for hours; some come every day, others once in a while. Both librarians consider it a good strategy for attracting and motivating readers; they feel it is good that the facility is used in this way.

The Norwood library is widely used by community members from very different backgrounds, and like the reference library, the selection of daily newspaper and magazines attracts a number of readers. The library is in the process of initiating more contact with the neighbourhood schools. The "Friends of the Library" is a fundraising support structure. For years, the "Friends of the Library" have collected second hand books, and always on the first Saturday of the month, a book sale is held on the library premises. In addition, community members sell tea, coffee, home-made cookies, cakes and other goodies. The proceeds of the book sale go to the library to acquire new books. There is usually a fairly good turnout, and people enjoy browsing through the books and having a chat.

The librarian argues that with the transition came a huge ideological change, and it was quite a challenge to get appropriate books on history or culture. At the beginning of the new South Africa, these resources were limited because, for example, history books that were not biased like apartheid era books were not yet written. There are only a few books in African languages available. The selection policy at the moment focuses on Africa because the library has a good selection of world literature but books from Africa were obviously neglected. There are book clubs in the neighbourhood, but there is no direct contact and they are private, by invitation only. It would be a nice project to launch a book club from the library. In both libraries, the common interest in reading and books brings community members from different backgrounds together.

In conclusion, the City Council and the Department of Community Development have a genuine interest in reviving neighbourhoods and promoting integration, but the

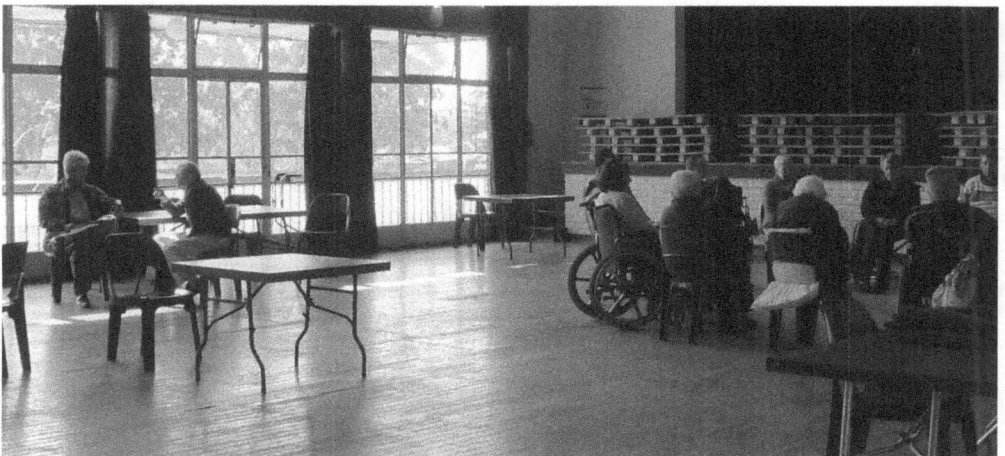

Fig. 13: Stroke Aid Self-Help Group Patterson Park Recreation Centre

context is one of limited resources, constrained state capacity, conflicting interests and contested strategies. Moreover, communication is difficult, because there are barely any community structures, local shops or public transport stops used by the majority of community members, where information could be disseminated. Currently, unequal power relations dictate local processes and determine the political agenda and priorities. Law, order and control dominate community engagement, and due to unacceptably high levels of crime, safety and security are high on the agenda. Decentralisation, limited state presence, the weight of the private sector and the power differential between the various population groups influence community development and the management of conflicts; less powerful population groups are marginalised and victimised. The roots of problems such as income distribution and unemployment are not addressed. Legislation is used to remove problems from the two neighbourhoods instead of addressing them.

4 Local Communities and the Ambiguity of Transformation

Introduction

Community and local public institutions are important agents in decentralised political structures. They have a certain representative function, interact with the local polity and city administration and potentially exert pressure on the government. Some political scientists argue that interaction and cooperation with local political institutions increases government responsiveness, transparency and accountability. This chapter discusses social networks and social organisations in Norwood and Orange Grove. Since only a limited number of social networks and organisations overlap with the specific geographical locality of the two neighbourhoods, I included social structures that have a stake in the community and are involved in public life: namely, the Community Police Forum (CPF), the residents' associations, the business organisations, the ward committees and the political parties. Unlike for example sports clubs, self-help organisations or choirs, these organisations engage with the state and the public administration. They are concerned with infrastructure development and maintenance, social and public life in the community and problems such as crime and disorder. In short, these organisations are concerned with issues affecting social interactions and quality of life in the two neighbourhoods. Moreover, these organisations are confronted with changes that are consequences of the transition. The nature of their engagement, their priorities and their concerns reveal their attitudes, willingness and capacity to adapt to the transformation. The ward councillors and ward committees are elected and have a legal mandate, in contrast to the CPF, the residents' associations and the business organisations.

This chapter also includes the Italian and Greek immigrant organisations because a considerable number of immigrants live in the two neighbourhoods. Immigrant organisations are based on the common descent of their members, which influences social structures and interactions. Immigrant organisations interact with political and administrative institutions, and they provide valuable insights into levels of integration and accommodation of diversity. Moreover, immigrant communities and their institutions potentially offer an alternative to public institutions and deficient state structures.

Urban development in post-apartheid Johannesburg had to address the legacies of racial segregation and the fragmentation of residential patterns produced by apartheid. This process of integration was complicated by the re-incorporation of South Africa into the global economy. Globalisation and the structural changes of the post-industrial labour market aggravated social polarisation, socio-economic inequalities and social divisions that operate not only along racial but also along class lines (Beall et al. 2002:30–31). The promotion and accommodation of diversity, as depicted in the metaphor of the "rainbow nation", were government strategies to unite a divided population and construct a new national identity.

Edwards and Foley state that civil society broadly has three different functions. Firstly, civil society structures have a socialisation function in building citizenship skills and influencing attitudes towards civic engagement. Secondly, civil society has a public and quasi-public function in providing certain services and necessities through voluntary organisations that complement or are a substitution for state welfare institutions. Finally, civil society has a representative or confrontational function by stimulating debates, disseminating information and offering a structure for interest aggregation (Edwards and Foley 2001:5–6). Moreover, there are two different ways to interact with the state: civil society can engage with the state or challenge and confront the state (Foley and Edwards 1996:39–40). Many different civil societies exist, and they originated as a variety of responses to the social, political and economic environment (Edwards and Foley 1998:124). Their space of agency, bargaining leverage and access to resources and power vary considerably.

Hall argues that the prospects of success from civic engagement are unevenly distributed between the different population groups, because social structures not only differ in terms of resources they are able to access but also in terms of the impact of their interventions on public life. Social interactions in civil societies tend to marginalise the working class, women, the young and the old. Social stratification and socio-economic class also inform social life, and many working class people rely on informal networks of friends and family (Hall 2002:52–56). In post-apartheid South Africa, informal survival networks among the poor and homeless produce considerable levels of social and mutual support structures; however, they are marginalised or excluded from political processes and often protest is the only political recourse they have. On the local level, effective strategies to address inequalities are limited and conflictual because wealthier groups are concerned with preserving the distributive arrangements that privilege them (Boix and Poser 1998:688). Moreover, affluent groups are linked to more powerful networks. The benefits emanating from social resources critically influence the options and bargaining leverage of dominant social groups, enabling them to undermine changes.

According to Krishna, even formal networks of the poor lack space of agency and control over political processes to make their voices heard. They exert less pressure on government and administrative structures than resourceful and powerful civil society structures.

Hence, there is a danger in decentralised political structures that privileged groups with a specific agenda represent the community at the expense of the poor and less powerful (Krishna 2002:25). In addition, community engagement may also facilitate and sustain personal client networks and patronage systems (Mosse 2001:29). In post-apartheid South Africa, divisions between different interest groups in communities are deep, so Robinson argues it is critical that any participatory community approaches address and mediate these tensions (Robinson 2006:131). Inclusive approaches to community development have to set norms that encourage and sustain the promotion of public interests beyond private or group-specific aspirations (Huysseune 2003:227).

A further problem is the lack of interest to get involved in the community by the majority of the population. This increases the danger that community based organisations work in favour of dominant individuals or groups and as they are more visible, they are also often accepted as legitimate representatives of the community by government institutions. In addition, there is a lack of communication structures in communities, where local schools and local shops are replaced by private schools and shopping malls. The former CPF chairperson in Norwood argued that the apathy of South Africans is disgusting. By way of example, he mentioned the many affluent people that have bought a townhouse that costs more than half a million, but they would not contribute to a community structure, not even 10 Rand a year or personally invest in their own future by getting involved in the community. The low levels of involvement increase the danger that exclusive community based organisations or well-resourced individuals dominate political and social interactions and potentially promote a particular agenda.

Heller stresses that in order to assess the possibilities and limitations of decentralisation, it is important to identify the institutional and socio-political arrangements that provide the context for interactions between different agents and interests. Successful decentralisation processes depend critically on the capacity of the central state because decentralisation requires coordination between different government tiers and regulations to ensure transparency and accountability. The space for effective and inclusive participatory structures is essential. Decentralisation only extends and deepens democratic structures in inclusive public political processes that integrate disadvantaged and marginalised groups (Heller 2001:138–140). There is a tendency that government and administrative structures engage with highly visible, articulate and dominant local structures, privileging them at the expense of more informal and less visible groups. Moreover, sustained partnerships with state institutions also provide a degree of legitimacy, which has the potential of being awarded to local structures that are not representative (Caulkins 2004:179).

Furthermore, perceptions of the state and the legitimacy of institutions shape the social environment, because the values and norms that inform political processes form the foundation of political trust and influence associational activities. (Harriss 2002:120). The state and the political and institutional context not only encourage levels of mobilisation and civic engagement, they also contribute to the development of collective agendas, shared objectives and goals as well as the promotion of tolerance and political trust in the context of diversity and cultural complexity that characterise modern societies (Foley and Edwards 1999:160–162). State capacity is fundamental to the quality of government performance; community structures and their engagement do not exist independently from the institutional context. Political instability, unpredictability of legislative processes, high levels of crime, biased law enforcement and corruption contribute to instability and a volatile political and economic environment, which affects social relations and interactions in local communities (Chhibber 2000:297–302, 308). Cooperation and social interactions are less conflictual in more egalitarian societies, and levels of social trust and tolerance are higher (Wuthnow 2002:86–87). Intolerance is linked to insecurity and exacerbated by socio-economic inequalities.

According to Colletta and Cullen, social cohesion and tolerance develop in the absence of latent conflict. Racial tensions, socio-economic inequalities, gender relations or disparities in political representation and participation are all latent conflicts, that potentially aggravate them. Moreover, social cohesion depends on social networks that cut across social divisions, on the presence of conflict management structures and on state institutions that are fair, transparent and accountable. Not only inequality, indignity and exclusion but also poor governance exacerbate social tensions and stimulate and sustain conflict (Colletta and Cullen 2000:12–16). Gibson and Gouws emphasise that the belief in democratic institutions and processes grows if they are not discriminatory and provide opportunities for all citizens to articulate their preferences (Gibson and Gouws 2003:46). Hence standards of impartiality, transparency and accountability in government and its institutions critically influence the quality of the social, economic and political environment that informs social dynamics and cooperation in local communities (Rothstein and Stolle 2003:194). The current distribution of power and the dominance of the ANC affect commitments to accountability, transparency and the responsiveness to local demands.

The Community Police Forum

Crime is a common concern and affects all the different population groups. Nevertheless, as Shaw argues, poor people are disproportionately affected and crime has a strong racial component regarding the perception of victims and perpetrators (Shaw 2002:50). Perceptions of safety and security affect levels of trust, impact interactions with other people and strangers, inform perceptions of acceptable behaviour and stimulate neighbourhood measures of control (Uslaner 2002:89). Sociability is influenced by the threat of crime: as Altbeker argues, crime increases social bonds and solidarity but also creates patterns of exclusion (Altbeker 2005:224–225). The violation of social norms by the police during apartheid contributed to the loss of the police's legitimacy which was exacerbated by the collapse of social control structures and weak law enforcement during the transition. The various population groups react differently to the breakdown of law and order. Depending on the availability of resources, strategies range from a resort to vigilantism and people's courts to privatised security. The variety of popular responses to the state's inability to effectively combat crime and violence undermine the state's monopoly of coercion and exclusive control over the justice system (Nell 2001:269–270). Crime is a common concern; nevertheless, the question arises whether the local population is united in the fight against crime or whether social barriers and racialised perceptions of crime are divisive.

Levels of crime and violence are a problem in South Africa. The budget reflects the prioritisation of the fight against crime. In 2004, the government spent 3 per cent of GDP on criminal justice in comparison to a worldwide average of only 1 per cent of the GDP. Nevertheless, this budget does not translate into more security and less crime; in contrast to a worldwide average of 380 police deployed per 100 000 people, only 260 police are deployed in South Africa, and they are not very visible (anonymous, Economist 2006). Besides the inefficient use of allocated resources, levels of corruption within the police force and the incapacity of the legal system to manage the number of court cases further undermine trust in the government's capacity to address and significantly reduce the problem of crime.

From the 1990s onwards, a number of community initiatives have emerged in response to the intolerable levels of crime and violence. According to Shaw, community policing became a central strategy to improve the strained relationship between the police and citizens (Shaw 2002:31). Community Police Fora (CPF) operate within the institutional context of the state, and it is the obligation and responsibility of police station commanders to initiate and convene meetings with the local community. In CPF meetings, the local population has the opportunity to discuss security concerns and become active partners in crime prevention (Schaerf et al. 2001:68). Community participation allows the assessment of the population's priorities and concerns, makes police more visible and increases transparency and accountability. The cooperation between the police and the population improves mutual relations, and participation in a CPF provides a sense of agency (Nell 2001:278). According to the chairperson of the Gauteng Provincial CPF, the provincial umbrella organisation, the cooperation between the police and the population and the active participation in the CPF reduces levels of crime. Despite encouraging results, a number of problems affect the cooperation between the police and the local population. In formerly white neighbourhoods, people are not really committed, give up on safety and security, perceive crime as out of hand, become apathetic and often have private security. However, privatised security does not address the roots of crime and violence but tries to drive crime away from a specific area to another. Only a few community members are involved, and there is the danger that CPFs become exclusive organisations as was nearly the case in the Norwood CPF. There is a lack of funding, and the government makes promises that do not materialise, for example increasing the visibility of the police. The police is not keen on the cooperation with the community and try to avoid at all costs the local population monitoring their commitment to the community and crime prevention. Moreover, organised crime has infiltrated the police, and political appointments purposely obstruct the system and functioning of the CPFs. According to the chairperson, the personnel in the provincial Department of Community Safety and in the police services is known to rather promote changes and strategies to marginalise and limit the influence of the CPFs. These personnel belong to the very same structures that decide on and implement these changes. Hence, these governmental structures "can turn things around in their favour" because there is no way to interfere, and changes are beyond the control of political institutions, for example local political

Fig. 14: Norwood Police Station

structures. Another huge problem is the criminal justice system. It is frustrating for the police to arrest people and, due to the limited capacity of the courts and law enforcement agencies, see arrested offenders quickly released again, sometimes on the same day (interview 2008). The state not only offers space for popular participation; the state can also limit or undermine civil society (Huysseune 2003:226). In the context of the CPFs, the state encourages community involvement and provides the formal rules that apply to the different social structures. But at the same time, the state also undermines participatory structures to prevent challenges and confrontations that expose the questionable interests of specific groups close to the state.

Norwood Police Station serves a larger area than the two neighbourhoods included in this study and has a good reputation. According to a survey conducted in 2004 by *Business Against Crime*, the station was the top station in Gauteng province, scoring 74.9 per cent for client service in contrast to the lowest station scoring 46.5 per cent. Station detectives scored 61.4 per cent in contrast to the 32.4 per cent of the worst performing stations, and victim support scored 96.1 per cent in comparison to 28.8 per cent (Mahlangu 2004).

Personnel replacements already starting in the 1990s also resulted in demographic shifts. Today, most of the police force is non-white including the current station commander. Many long-term residents are upset about this development, and there is a general perception that the quality of police services has dramatically declined. In 2006, there was a lot of resentment and mobilisation against the new Norwood Police Station commander, which was also prompted by the fact that she is both female and black. In addition, community members involved in the CPF are white while the police are mostly black. The racial divisions between the two structures are even more problematic considering the racialised perceptions of crime.

The Norwood CPF holds monthly meetings where crime statistics are presented reflecting types of crime and numbers of arrests, problem areas are identified and strategies to combat crime developed. The police and the CPF organise information and crime prevention events including information evenings at the Paterson Park Recreation Centre, an information table at a local mall, crime prevention courses for domestic staff and crime awareness drives. The apathy of community members is a problem. The cooperation with the community includes the local schools and institutions of faith on an individual level; nobody from these institutions attends the monthly meetings. A victim support structure is linked to the police station, and community volunteers are trained for this task. Lifeline, the trauma counselling centre in Norwood, works closely with the CPF's victim support service; Lifeline also provides training for new trauma counsellors. The CPF also has a fairly good media presence in the North Eastern Tribune, the local newspaper that is distributed to all households.

The focus of the CPF goes beyond crime prevention, and recurring problems that are discussed at each meeting are illegal bars and liquor licences, drug trafficking and prostitution along Louis Botha, homeless people and hawkers in the area and the legal and illegal taxi ranks. The cooperation with the liquor board is a problem. A number of bars would not qualify for a liquor licence; however, the liquor board can issue temporary licences and tends to renew them indefinitely in exchange for bribes. The different facilities and people that fall outside of the social norm are considered a threat to the community because there is a consensus among residents that they increase the risk of crime. Nevertheless, there is a racial dimension to these issues because they are experienced as problems of whites that are caused by blacks.

Membership numbers of the CPF fluctuate, but there is a core group of about ten committed people, all of them white. There are 162 reservists who are trained community members that support the police, for example as additional manpower at road blocks (minutes of CPF meeting on 30/1/2008). Currently all reservists are white. The chairperson of the CPF and the members of the executive committee are elected at the Annual General Meeting (AGM). The AGM in May 2007 had to face several problems. On 23 May 2007, the AGM attracted about 60 community members and also included non-white community members. These community members were mainly from the police barracks, a block of flats behind the police station that provides accommodation for police personnel and their families. As the meeting was about to start, the lights went off and there was no electricity, so the meeting was postponed for a week. On 30 May 2007, the turnout was nearly as good as the week before and again racially more integrated, and the electricity supply did not cause any problems. Since the CPF is a government structure, the meeting was also attended by Monde Ntebe of Gauteng's Provincial Department of Community Safety.

There were problems with the preparation of the AGM. For example the audited financial statement were unavailable, which violated the by-laws. It prompted a community member to interfere because it is impossible to discharge and elect a new treasurer without the approval of the financial statements. This intervention caused irritation among the members of the executive committee. Monde Ntebe saved the situation by suggesting that if there are no irregularities, the community can authorise the approval of the audited statement by the new executive committee. Nevertheless, the problems continued because the old executive committee was standing again for re-election. The process of nomination was a problem because the community lacks the social structures to inform community members and call for nominations. Usually, the AGM is announced in the North Eastern Tribune, and there are posters and pamphlets at the Norwood Police Station calling for nominations, but apparently nobody responded. The lack of nominations prompted the members of the executive committee to nominate themselves, a fact that was criticised by Monde Ntebe. This intervention resulted in a dispute: members of the executive committee argued that they sacrifice time to do a job that obviously no other community members are willing to do and that Monde's intervention is completely out of place. During a very agitated discussion in which Monde tried to negotiate, two coloured ladies from the floor suggested that under the current circumstances, the executive committee could just as well elect themselves and not bother asking community members to attend the AGM. Monde was accused of filibustering the meeting, and community members walked out in protest. In the end, the old executive committee was re-elected (AGM 30 May 2007). The chairperson of the CPF and the provincial CPF chairperson both considered Monde's intervention outrageous and argued that Monde should not have attended in the first place.

Division among members of the executive committee started to surface centering around the new station commander and rumours that criminal charges were laid against her. The one faction, headed by a very prominent community member, who is also the chairperson of the Orange Grove Residents' Organisation, wanted the new station commander out but they did not want to respect legal procedures. The chairperson of the CPF stressed the imperative of adhering to legal procedure; however, the problem resulted in an ugly dispute that was very disruptive to the CPF and ended with the resignation of some executive committee members. According to these former executive committee members, the CPF has collapsed and they motivated an article in the local paper, the *North Eastern Tribune,* that highlighted problems with the taxi ranks and suggested that the problems were not being properly addressed. In *The Star*, the Johannesburg daily newspaper, a further article criticised the situation at the police barracks including overcrowding, heaps of garbage, disintegration of the building infrastructure, lack of supervision of children and the police's negligence of the problem. The article demanded an urgent intervention.

In contrast, the newly elected chairperson of the CPF initiated a number of changes and the work of the CPF improved and became more visible, which attracted a few new members. The unemployed wife of a police officer from the police barracks, was employed by the CPF to do administrative work. Different working committees were established: one to deal with the different security companies in the community, one to establish a crèche for the children in the police barracks and one to organise a soccer team in the community, including the children from the police barracks, to participate in the different activities that framed the Soccer World Cup in 2010. These activities continue and also include the maintenances of the premises around the police barracks. The CPF also organised a replacement for the police station receptionist on maternity leave, better equipped the station board room and refurbished the victim counselling room. The CPF followed up on complaints and on missing dockets. At the monthly meetings, not only the number of arrests but also the number of convictions were presented. A designated member of the executive committee was in charge of complaints against members of the police. However, there was a problem with groundless complaints voiced by community members out of anger; afterwards, it was difficult to hold people accountable. These unjustified attacks on the quality of the police services became a problem because they reduced levels of trust. As a consequence, the executive committee decided to only honour complaints put in writing. Finally, the CPF introduced a reward system to motivate the police. Every month, the best performing cop and the cop confiscating the highest number of firearms receive an award and a voucher sponsored by the business community.

One of the changes initiated by the CPF chairperson nearly went horribly wrong. In order to address the problem of legal and illegal taxi ranks, the owners of the taxi companies operating in the area were invited to the monthly CPF meeting. According to the CPF chairperson, this was a first ever in the history of CPFs (CPF meeting 30 January 2008). A working committee cooperated with the taxi owners and tried to involve them in the development of sustainable solutions, but after an initial commitment, the taxi owners increasingly failed to attend the meetings. On 28 March 2008, a stringent law enforcement operation by the Metro Police – the police structure in charge of traffic in Johannesburg – established road blocks at different intersections along Louis Botha Avenue. The Metro Police was backed by a strong contingent of the South African Police Services, the Gauteng Province Traffic Patrol Unit, Emergency Management Services, reservists and CPF members. As a result of the operation, 39 taxis were impounded and the illegal taxi ranks closed. In the evening, frustrated taxi drivers mobilised against the chairperson of the CPF. They found out where he lived and arrived at his house. He immediately alerted the police station in Norwood, but nobody came to his rescue and no case was opened against the taxi drivers. The CPF chairperson managed to leave his home with his family and stayed at a friend's house for the night. As a result, he acknowledged that it is impossible to win the war with the taxi industry, and the cooperation was abandoned (CPF meeting 28 May 2008).

The racial composition of CPF members is a problem, as there are hardly any non-white people participating. One black community member was involved in the CPF for a while. His participation was prompted by the confusion around the Astra Café on Louis Botha Avenue. The intolerable noise levels and the number of cars parked in front of garage entrances and on pavements were such a problem that the CPF was approached. With the support of the CPF it was possible to close down Astra Café. However, despite this success, this community member stated that it is not easy to be black in a white neighbourhood. His relationship with the two neighbours living next door to his property is good because they know each other personally and trust each other, but the rest of the neighbours are very distant. Moreover, there is a trend to involve black people in neighbourhood structures as it makes these organisations look good and integrated. However, in reality people are still alienated from each other and relations remain unfriendly and distant (interview 2008).

This community member was also concerned about the drug trafficking along Louis Botha and the rumours that members of the police from the Norwood Police Station are involved at the very least, or, they accept bribes in exchange for no interference or no prosecution. He argued that coming from a black community and knowing how relational networks operate among black people made it easy to pick up fraud and the mechanisms of patronage; it was really obvious that police personnel were involved. However, it seems this is another war impossible to win. Another community member wrote an open letter to the station commander and the CPF stating the problem of drug trafficking. There was no reaction but the letter created problems for the family of the complainant. In the end it was counter-productive and resulted for example in two blacks, huge guys, that were constantly positioned in the street in front of the complainant's property and were obviously observing his movements. Fear of the drug lords exacting revenge became too much of a threat to the family. This community member concluded that it is not worth speaking out and never attended any further CPF meetings because in the current political context, community involvement will not achieve anything (interview 2008).

The chairpersons of the local and provincial CPF did not negate the possible collusion between the police and the drug lords along Louis Botha. However, they argued that despite the evidence, it is imperative to follow the legal dismissal procedures. Despite the obvious involvement of at least some members of the police, they both had doubts about the direct involvement of the station commander. She is certainly aware of the problem but chooses to ignore it (CPF meeting 27 February 2008). The Councillor also has evidence of collusion between the police and drug lords, but states that it is impossible to intervene because the same police officers that would have to arrest the drug lords are also cooperating with them. Moreover, it is not even possible to resolve minor problems. For example, the Councillor approached the Metro Police because an illegal exhaust repair business had started operating on the pavement on Louis Botha Avenue. The Councillor expected the police to intervene, or at least to issue a fine and remove the business, but two days later saw the Metro Police using the repair facilities themselves (CPF meeting 27 February 2008).

At the beginning of August 2008, the Annual General Meeting (AGM) of the CPF was due. Invitations and calls for nominations were disseminated through the *North Eastern Tribune*, the Norwood Police Station and via email. Within a week the AGM was postponed and then two days later again confirmed at the previous date. The confusion continued up to the day of the AGM. Apparently, there was a problem with the chairperson, he was not present and nobody was prepared to go into details about it. Again there were organisational shortcomings including no nominations for the executive committee, hence people from the floor were nominated. Despite the chaos, Monde Ntebe chose not to intervene (AGM 7 August 2008). In order to save the situation, three members of the executive committee asked for suggestions from the audience to get a sense of the concerns and demands in the community and prepare for activities in the year ahead. A number of community members contributed with suggestions and were invited to join a working committee.

In an interview, the former chairperson of the CPF clarified the reasons for his disappearance. Provincial Police Commissioner Naidoo opened a case against him for inciting disorder, disruption and violence in connection with a planned march to protest poor police services from Sandringham Police Station to the offices of the provincial MEC of Safety and Security. Commissioner Naidoo assumed that the former chairperson was behind the planned march because he was once a member and reservist of the Sandringham CPF. This was not the case, but the opening of a docket and the impending court appearance prevented the nomination as chairperson of the CPF. As a CPF chairperson, he had a difficult relationship with Naidoo, because he was very persistent for example in following up on different very controversial issues. Months later the former CPF chairperson has not heard about or received any documents regarding the case that was opened against him. Moreover, the Norwood CPF is again struggling to survive (interview 2008).

The CPF is a good example of the complexity of local interactions. Transformation is a conscious commitment and not just a by-product of community engagement. Moreover, internalised behaviour patterns, alienation between the different community members and the lack of trust affect social interactions. The former CPF chairperson pointed at the considerable differences between people in the community. Some are afraid to speak up, do not question authorities and wait until someone tells them what to do. In contrast, assertive community members that are influential try to dominate the community. A big problem is how individuals react to the police: they do not take the police seriously and show disrespect and indignation. These attitudes are humiliating. Not only citizens but also the police are frustrated with the justice system: people are arrested but immediately released, which is a disincentive for the police to invest a lot of effort into their work. Community engagement also depends on the support of political structures that fulfil their obligations and have a commitment to cooperation with the community. Finally, safety and security and the prevention of crime are a contentious issue. There is a danger that the legitimate concern for personal safety is used to justify questionable actions that disrespect the rights and dignity of other citizens. Assumptions of the government's inefficiency, corruption and arrogant leadership to cover up failures enforce perceptions that citizens not only have the right to protection, but that they also have to do it themselves, which often results in measures that conflict with democratic rights.

Residents' Associations

Residents' Associations already existed during apartheid, and they are more popular than the ward committees. In fact, members of the residents' associations explicitly distance themselves from the ward committees because they do not want to be involved in politics and argue that ward committees are not necessary. The Norwood and Orchards Residents' Association (NORA) and the Orange Grove Residents' Association both have more than 200 members; however, only about 50 per cent pay the annual membership fees, and only a small group is actively involved (interviews 2006, 2007). Nevertheless, there was an opinion change regarding participation in ward committees and a few members of the Orange Grove Residents' Association made themselves available to the ward committee and participated in the ward committee elections in July 2006. The residents' associations are concerned with infrastructure maintenance and increasingly with challenges to law and order, in particular illegal businesses, hawking, homeless people in the area and crime prevention. The context of the residents' associations is one where the middle class feels increasingly powerless as it loses control with respect to the influx of homeless people, crime, declining commitment of residents and violations of regulations and by-laws. The cooperation within residents' associations is influenced by perceptions of the local environment, in particular levels of safety, security and order. A small group of long-time residents constitute the core group of NORA, while a very active and involved local resident is the driving force behind the Orange Grove Residents' Association.

Representation in changing communities is contested. Mansbridge distinguishes between descriptive representation, referring to visible characteristics and shared experiences, and substantive representation. Substantive representation is reflected in the deliberative function, for example the discussion of policies or programmes, and the aggregative function, for example canvassing of support that provides a degree of legitimacy (Mansbridge 2000:99–103). Social meanings of particular groups are historically constructed, tend to outlive social transformation and are often unconsciously reproduced through social practice. For example, population groups such as Africans or women that were legally excluded from the vote carry the stigma of being unfit to participate in politics and are under-represented in so called "representative" structures. Low or non-representation in turn reinforces perceptions that these groups are unfit to rule (Mansbridge 2000:119–120). In a context of contested space where privileges are linked to exclusion, the marginalisation of specific population groups serves not only to defend material interests but also extends to the validation of people deserving to live in the neighbourhood (Ballard 2004:50). Concerns around neighbourhood development potentially strengthen social structures that become increasingly exclusive and there is a correlation between group solidarity and intolerance in South Africa (Gibson and Gouws 2003:90). According to Wuthnow, social organisations that rather pursue specific interests distinguish themselves from organisations concerned with the public good because exclusive organisations also cause newcomers from specific population groups to feel unwelcome (Wuthnow 2002:79). As it is in general difficult to contact community members and motivate newcomers, most new contacts are made via the personal relations of existing members and patterns of information dissemination perpetuate the racial composition of the two residents' associations. On the other hand, there are for example more than two hundred non-white households living in the police barracks; however, according to the residents' associations it would not be an option to invite them to meetings, and most likley they also would not choose to come (interviews 2006, 2007).

Power relations are reflected in social hierarchies, and social networks reproduce them. Social hierarchies are also reflected within local structures and Molyneux argues that men tend to assume leadership positions or control financial resources, and women usually do not belong to networks that have economic spin-offs. (Molyneux 2002:180–181). Internal structures of social networks not only tend to favour men for leadership positions, but even if women are elected as chairpersons, they are less respected, more scrutinised and more criticised than men (Neuhouser 1995:52). Moreover, disparities between the number of men speaking at meetings and the number of women is a common characteristic of social interactions, and contributions by men often have more weight than those of women (Cleaver 2001:43). Heller argues that gender is still a significant barrier to equal participation: according to the attendance register of the South African National

Civic Organisations, women are disproportionately represented within local structures but under-represented in elected or leadership positions (Heller 2003:165).

A younger women, who had recently moved to the neighbourhood argued that she had a hard time as a new member of NORA. Inspired by the Oprah Winfrey show, she wanted to make a difference in the community and her neighbourhood a better place including speaking up in case of problems. In her early thirties she was younger than the average age of active NORA members and she complained about having difficulty in gaining respect particularly from elderly men and long-time residents. Every time she drew attention to problems in the community, no other NORA member was willing to get involved, on the contrary, she was told that she doesn't have to reinvent the wheel or that she is just preaching to the converted. There was neither support nor contributions with constructive suggestions (interview 2007, 2008).

A member of the Ward 74 ward committee argued in an interview that the Orange Grove Residents' Association is exclusively active in Orange Grove West, the part of Orange Grove that is located east of Louis Botha Avenue. A small group of the association initiated a plan to introduce private security in Orange Grove West, Fellside and Victoria. This initiative is not only a response to the poor service quality and unreliability of the Norwood Police Station. The City Improvement District planned along Louis Botha starts in Victoria and extends to Fellside and Orange Grove, so it augments the project in an ideal way by reducing the threats emanating from the current businesses and residents along Louis Botha. Residents of Orange Grove West, Victoria and Fellside were invited to a first meeting on 29 July 2008; although the police barracks are located in this area, no invitations were extended to these residents nor were residents along Louis Botha Avenue invited. About 30–40 people attended the meeting, certainly below the expectations of the organisers judging by the quantity of information material distributed on a much larger number of chairs. Not one non-white resident attended the meeting; the only two black attendants were officials from the City Council (meeting UMD launch 29 July 2008).

According to the organisers, the planned Urban Management District (UMD) is a dynamic network partnership of commercial and residential property owners. The specific exclusion of tenants from the UMD discriminates against certain residents and explains the omission of people living in the police barracks and residents living in flats along Louis Botha Avenue. The Louis Botha Business Association (LBBA) is an established Section 21 company (non-profit organisation) that will manage the UMD (meeting UMD launch 29 July 2008). The same person, already chairperson of the Orange Grove Residents' Associations, also chairs the LBBA. The UMD will work closely with the City Council,

Region E and the Greater Johannesburg Metro Council, and it aims at the improvement of the neighbourhood. According to the pamphlet distributed at the meeting, the UMD offers more security, makes the neighbourhood clean and proper, identifies bad buildings, acts against illegal land use and aims to remove hawkers and vagrants; all these measures increase the value of properties. A private security company will provide surveillance and assistance with clearly identifiable, highly trained security personnel patrolling the neighbourhoods, monitoring the streets and keeping them clean and orderly (pamphlet produced by the Orange Grove/Victoria/Fellside on the planned Urban Management District 2008). Apparently, if more than 51% of the property owners are participating in the UMD, the remaining property owners will have to accept the UMD as the representative structures and financially contribute toward it.

Business Organisations

Business used to have a vested interest in the social and political environment of business locations. This interest motivated local engagement and sponsorship of civil society structures and non-profit organisations to improve and sustain quality of life in neighbourhoods and reduce the potential for conflict. Heying debates the decline of social engagement of business elites. He argues that globalisation and the delocalisation of businesses have reduced the local engagement of the business sector, which has a direct impact on communities in a context of inadequate self-interests. Even if the local business representatives of the national or international corporate sector are established in a specific neighbourhood, they remain disconnected from the local community. There are no incentives for financial contributions to local institutions or the non-profit sector (Heying 2001:108–109). Furthermore, the concentration of shops and businesses in malls adds to the delocalisation of business from urban neighbourhoods, as the development in Norwood and Orange Grove also demonstrates. Residents increasingly use facilities located outside the two neighbourhoods for shopping and services. More personal relationships between customers and the local business sector decline. In contrast, business relations within the Muslim and Jewish communities as well as in specific immigrant communities favour their community members and strengthen social relations (interviews 2006, 2007).

Businesses also adapt to changing demographics and the demands of a new clientèle (Juergens et al. 2003:64–66). The two traditional healers on Louis Botha Avenue and hairdressers that straighten curly hair on Louis Botha and Grant Avenue are good examples of new services adapted to the demands of a more diversified population. These changes are in addition to the changing range of food available at the Spar supermarket,. According to the owner of the Spar supermarket, the selection in shops has changed: the shop caters not only for Whites and Jews, but increasingly for customers belonging to the black middle class and the Indian community (interview 2007).

The Grant Avenue Business Association engages with local political and social structures to revive Grant Avenue and make it more attractive. Safety and security are central aspects together with investment in infrastructure, clean streets and the enforcement of law and order. Contrasting interests of the different population groups and disagreement regarding the use of public space increase controversies and the potential for conflict. A recurring problem is the incapacity of the state to enforce law and order and the inadequate responses to the problem of informal businesses and the homeless.

A number of property owners along Grant Avenue are disinterested, and the lacking investment in the maintenance of buildings is a problem. In addition, not all property owners are concerned about the nature of the businesses on their premises; they seem not to care as long as the tenants pay the monthly rent. There are about 150 to 200 landlords and business owners along Grant Avenue; however, only six to eight people are driving the development of Grant Avenue. A City Improvement District (CID) plan was submitted to the government, which considered it a good project but at the same time stated

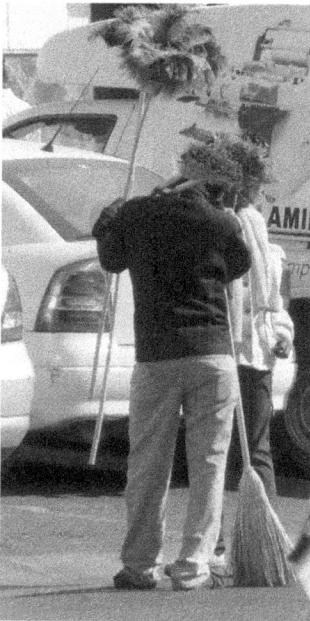

Figs. 15 and 16: Informal Traders near Spar and Woolworth

that there is no money for it. The only way to implement the project is to finance it with contributions from the private sector. According to one interview partner, the question arises of how one can expect businesses in this area to contribute to the CID and the law is then not enforced. In the end, this is a farce because there is no point in investing money if the government is not doing its job. In general, government services are a problem, the police do not respond to calls, social services do not come to remove the "vagrants" and the city does not act on problems. Business owners pay taxes and don't see what the city does with this money. In case of any problems, the businesses have to look for solutions themselves (interview 2007).

According to a member of NORA, an attempt to win the necessary number of land-lords and business owners to support the planned City Improvement District (CID) failed because less than the required 51 per cent agreed to the project. The Councillor, the Grant Avenue Business Association and NORA therefore started to approach ten-ants. They asked the tenants to engage with their landlords and encourage them to invest in the buildings and to support the CID. Nevertheless, the majority was not interested. The response to suggestions that local businesses contribute to the appearance of Grant Avenue with nice displays in their windows or a flower arrangement at shop entrances was disappointing (interview 2007).

The City Council's planned development of Grant Avenue as an activity street with a projected reduction of traffic in favour of a more pedestrian-friendly environment is criticised and considered neither a viable project nor an effective strategy for reviving Grant Avenue. To reduce traffic in Grant Avenue is a problem because a public bus ser-vice runs along Grant Avenue, and it is impossible to change this. Moreover, if Grant Avenue is closed to traffic, there is a problem with the trucks that deliver merchandise to Woolworths and Spar. These trucks would have to use roads in residential areas, creating a lot of resistance from local residents. There is also no confidence in the government's capacity to implement this project. Even if these changes are introduced, it would be dif-ficult to attract patrons, for example in the evening if there are people sleeping in front of the restaurants on the pavements (interview 2007). Local bars that attract the younger generation would profit from a more pedestrian-friendly Grant Avenue. Nevertheless, younger people are not included in the development plans of the Grant Avenue Busi-ness Association because bars are considered to contribute to the disintegration of the neighbourhood and not to the revival of Grant Avenue. This example not only reveals generational conflicts in community development processes but also the weight of local elites in setting standards for development programmes by excluding a potentially suc-cessful sector.

Business activities along Louis Botha Avenue are a mixture of formal and informal structures, which impacts on the cooperation methods between the various enterprises.

Informal businesses rely on informal social relations that are not necessarily visible to outsiders, and they are not invited to join local business associations. The Louis Botha Business Association (LBBA) is not interested in contacts with more informal businesses, and hence the majority of businesses along Louis Botha are excluded from the business association. On the contrary, the LBBA plans to evict these businesses and rehabilitate the area. Most of the buildings are declared "bad-building areas" by the City Council. Government intervention will target these buildings and eventually evict the current residents and businesses (Interviews 2007 and 2008). The impact of the City Improvement District (CID) is already visible in the rehabilitation of the building complex at the corner of Louis Botha Avenue and Osborne Road. This complex includes the Victory Theatre, apartments and business facilities. The comprehensive renovation has changed the demographic composition of residents and the nature of businesses. Improved security aims to attract a different clientèle, which is reflected in new restaurants and shops and their

Figs. 17 and 18: Shops on Louis Botha

more affluent middle class patrons. At the same time, unwanted population groups and businesses have been removed from the area.

Due to limited government resources, public-private partnerships are promoted for the rehabilitation of Louis Botha Avenue. According to a ward committee member this strategy results in plans for expensive apartments in the rehabilitated buildings because the private sector is not concerned with the social aspects of development. Nevertheless, it would create huge problems and violence would erupt if the current residents are evicted from the buildings (interview 2008). The projected city improvement along Louis Botha Avenue is therefore another example of the marginalisation of less powerful population groups. Moreover, distrust in the efficiency of the state to respond to local demands encourages private local development initiatives (Mohan 2001:163). Space is political. A comprehensive policy approach has to reconcile the allocation of space with the socio-economic organisation of society and the diversity and complexity of interests and needs (Lefebvre 1976:33, 35). In Johannesburg, according to Murray, power has shifted from the state to a diversity of networks that are dominated by the vested interests of powerful population groups, the corporate sector and estate agents. This constellation results in the restructuring of the city into fragmented and privatised zones (Murray 2008:46). The development along Louis Botha is constructed as a legitimate concern for city development, but it simultaneously serves to remove population groups that are not welcome in the neighbourhood. The promotion of public-private partnerships reduces the option of government intervention in favour of the poor and perpetuates inequalities.

Local Political Structures

Unequal power relations are conducive to tensions and conflict (Robinson 2006:139). Consequently, the distribution of power is critical to understanding local politics. Power operates in different ways and determines not only who has access to resources, but also who influences local politics, sets the agenda, determines problems and decides on the allocation of resources. Power is a resource of individuals, groups and institutions. Power relations are dynamic because different individuals or groups exercise power in different spaces and at different times. Power has a cultural dimension that results in specific power hierarchies. Finally, power is often elusive and hidden (Watson 1999:214). Power is central to local politics; hence, it is important to focus on the function, objectives and aspirations of different civil society structures to assess the significant disparities between different social networks and associations (Prakash and Selle 2004:21). Moreover, individuals with a good education, professional success, leadership skills and a strong personality have much higher levels of self-confidence, trust and civic competence. These individuals tend to dominate social life and potentially use social structures for personal goals (Dekker 2004:103). This section on local political structures is divided into two parts. The first discusses elected local institutions, the ward committees and the ward councillor. The second part discusses the two most popular political parties operating in the two neighbourhoods.

The Ward Committees

In July 2006, Ward 73 and Ward 74 held ward committee elections. Ward committees should represent the population of the ward in terms of racial composition and geographical areas. Ward committees are the mediating structure between the councillor and the community: members of the ward committee participate in community activities and are aware of problems and concerns of the citizenry, which are then discussed with the councillor and if necessary, presented to the City Council. The individual ward committee member has a specific portfolio. The ten portfolios are safety, housing, infrastructure, planning and development, finance and economic development, community development, corporate support and administration, health, transport and environment. Ward committee elections are a problem because it is difficult to find ten community members who are willing to stand for election. It is even more challenging to nominate enough people to comply with the requirements of representation and offer a choice to the electorate. The lack of information channels contributes to an extremely uneven distribution of information regarding the call for nominations and the announcement of the ward committee elections. According to the former ward councillor support of Ward 73 and 74, the process of nominations is unclear and the low turnout is a problem. Ward councillors decide on the election venue, and there are advertisements in the local newspapers, for example the *North Eastern Tribune* or the *Rosebank and Killarney Post*. Nevertheless, the most effective mobilisation occurs through the various networks of the political parties. Ward councillors are in a powerful position and tend to approach people they would like to have in the ward committee. The city is planning a civic education programme because many citizens do not know how local government structures work (interview 2006).

The lack of popular participation is a problem. According to Mattes, South Africa has the most passive citizenry in Southern Africa. Different factors contribute to low levels of civic engagement. The question arises whether political processes and the institutional context are conducive to civic engagement in South Africa and offer a genuine space in political processes for an active citizenry. Participation requires institutions that encourage meaningful participation and give citizens a reason to participate (Mattes 2002:32–34). Costa and Kahn argue that heterogeneity, in particular income inequality and a high Gini Coefficient are negatively correlated to levels of civic engagement (Costa and Kahn 2001: 31–33). Moreover, participation is linked to dignity. People that are excluded from the labour market and live in a highly volatile socio-economic context refrain from becoming involved in the community. In contrast, exclusive social networks that pursue a particular agenda tend to make unwanted population groups feel irrelevant (Wuthnow 2002:79). Finally, the promotion of popular participation ignores the complexity of political processes in a context where people are dissatisfied with the government, feel suspicious of the way politics is conducted and have slim chances of influencing politics (Paterson 2000:39).

The Councillor states that political involvement still happens outside the formal political structures: people are interested and engaged in politics but do not try to be elected into official political structures. The problem is that people complain and when asked what they would do about it, they still don't want to get involved in politics. For example there are complaints about Louis Botha Avenue but nobody is aware that it is necessary to get involved in order that things start happening. In addition, according to the Councillor, apartheid had so many prohibitions, it invited violations. Now the situation has changed, but people still think that if they do not agree with a rule or a law they can ignore it. Even worse, it seems that some people think that with democracy they can do what they want and disrespect the law. The isolation during apartheid and the structure of the authoritarian state also contributed to a situation where people often do not question anything, do not have their own opinion on a particular issue or take a decision themselves because during apartheid the state did think for them (interview 2006).

In July 2006, the ward committee election of Ward 74 attracted few interested people. In fact, ten people attended, including the Councillor and a city council official to monitor the elections. The people attending were all elected into the committee and also constituted the electorate. The new ward committee members included DA and three ANC members. After the elected people presented themselves, they were asked whether they accept their election. A first meeting of the new ward committee with the Councillor was scheduled two weeks later at the beginning of August (ward committee elections Ward 74, 19 July 2006).

One day later, the ward committee elections of Ward 73 attracted even less people, seven people attended the meeting including the Councillor and the city official. Again the people attending were asked whether they would accept their election; they did not even present themselves (ward committee elections Ward 73, 20 July 2006).

The ward committee of Ward 73 and the Councillor are mainly concerned with problems in the ward, such as repairs to infrastructure or enforcement of law and order, and not with development projects in the community. According to the Councillor, there is in any case no money available, and it is already difficult to mobilise the resources to resolve problems and maintain infrastructure. The Councillor stressed that she works closely with the different organisations in the community: the CPF, NORA, the Grant Avenue Business Association and the schools. According to the Councillor, the most challenging problems are safety, security, crime prevention and the hawkers and "vagrants" in the area (interview 2006). Zoleka Zide, the new ward councillor support for Ward 73, is very well informed about the City Council's Integrated Development Framework but argued that there are not a lot of problems in Ward 73: the infrastructure is developed in contrast to other wards. Zide stated that she has a good relationship with the Councillor (interview with Zide 2008).

David Mawelewele, the new ward councillor support for Ward 74, is not as well informed and organised as Zoleka Zide. His office looks like a wholesale storage room with cartons of long-life milk, boxes of cookies and Coca Cola can trays. He forgot about the scheduled interview and had to make a number of telephone calls before we could start. Mawelewele stated that the cooperation with the Councillor is good; there are no problems. Ward 74 is in a wealthy area, so there are only small projects planned: street lights and toilets for one of the public parks (interview with Mawelewele 2008).

The ward committee of Ward 74 is very active. However, a ward committee member from the ANC states that people in the ward committee have actually joined out of personal interest. They have their own agenda, and they are not promoting the interests of the community in the ward committee. There is a lot going on behind closed doors. There are complaints that ward committee members do not come to the meetings but often not everyone is invited to meetings or invitations arrive so late that one already has another commitment. The Councillor is biased and told one of the ANC members after the ward committee election that the ANC membership is not a problem but that she has to be aware that it is a DA ward and that the interests of the DA constituency are promoted (interview 2008). The Councillor stated that she is not keen to have the ANC represented in the ward committee (interview 2006). Another ward committee and ANC member also stated that he is not very integrated in the ward committee. There is a core group, and not everyone receives all the information (interview 2006). Peter Monyuku, the former ward councillor support, stated that ward councillors are powerful, and there is little control and accountability. An institutional reform is planned where councillors will be supervised and controlled by the office of the speaker of the City Council. Currently, councillors are supervised and accountable to the chief whip of their own political party (interview with Monyuku 2006).

Ward committee members of the ANC stress that there is one ward committee member with more information than any other community member. This is an advantage for the respective person and apparently, he is a gate-keeper and in a positions to manipulate processes. He is involved everywhere in the Orange Grove Residents' Association, in the ward committee, in the Louis Botha Business Association, and in the Urban Management District and in the Paterson Park development. Nobody knows exactly what he is doing and where he is involved ultimately. Not only is he involved in the Paterson Park Development but also in the rehabilitation of the Paterson Park Recreation Centre, and then not only as ward committee member and member of the Orange Grove Residents' Association but also with his business (interview 2008). This is on the one hand a good example of commendable community involvement and on the other hand it exemplifies how the lack of local participation and the lacking oversight by political institutions may result in the promotion of a particular non-inclusive agenda by a small powerful community group or individual.

One ANC members also pointed at the less obvious dynamics in the ward committee. Not all committee members are taken seriously and are rarely asked for their opinion. They are in charge of the less important ward committee portfolio in a middle class neighbourhood, for example the health portfolio that is concerned with public health facilities in the ward. Moreover, not all ANC ward committee members have a car which causes transport problems to attend ward committee meetings at the Region E offices in Sandton (interview 2008).

The Political Parties
The two most prominent political parties in Norwood and Orange Grove are not very active. The DA has a ward branch in Ward 73, but nobody organises any events (interview 2006). The two parties admit that they are mainly visible in the two communities during election campaigns. The ANC has ward branches: Ward 73 and Ward 74 together constitute one branch. According to an ANC member, the new structure of the ANC in Johannesburg does not work as it has 109 branches that correspond with the local government wards. There are too many wards, which is beyond the organisational capacity of the party. Moreover, there is the inexperience of the ANC in government, reflected for example in the difficulties to implement policies. The problem is also that the ANC had to start from a dysfunctional and plundered state in 1994 and at the same time there were the high expectations of the population (interview 2006). There are monthly branch

meetings, but they are not very well attended. Civil society structures have achieved a lot during the struggle, but the topics have changed today, problems for example are street lights that don't work or a pavement that needs repair. The ANC tries to address the problem of crime or unemployment and tries to find a solution for the hawkers and homeless people. The branch considers the reintroduction of house meetings to discuss more fundamental issues; house meetings were popular during the struggle. The branches are not very active and hence, there are not many organised events. The branches have to increase their visibility in order to attract new members (interview 2006).

Another ANC member stresses that it is difficult to reach people and mobilise the ANC constituency. There is a new dynamic among domestic workers in the area; their social networks in the community have changed and the community looks different today. During the struggle the ANC had different structures and domestic workers were interested and engaged in the community. This has changed and people haven't found a new political home yet. Domestic workers still experience many problems. There is a government set minimum wage, and they should have an employment contract. However, many domestic workers have unacceptable working conditions, but if they complain and demand their rights, they are fired. They do not receive the necessary support from the local ANC structures. Moreover, there is no continuity and few relationships among domestic workers as they have high mobility levels. There are also concerns on the local level about the future of the ANC, especially levels of corruption are worrying. Many councillors just want the money in their pockets, they don't care about delivery and there is a lack of accountability (interview 2008).

One ANC member pointed at the ambiguity of the ANC's code of conduct around controversial issues and argued that a certain alignment is necessary as well as loyalty to the party but not blind loyalty; there is also freedom of speech. There are disciplinary measures but it was not necessary to resort to them in the two local branches. On the local levels, national politics are discussed at the branch meetings but once they are decided everyone has to defend the ANC line even if one personally does not agree (interview with 2006).

Immigrant Organisations

Social networks are useful and offer support structures to immigrants that are confronted with a different way of life in their host countries. Levels of integration vary between and within immigrant groups, and they depend not only on the social environment of the neighbourhood but also on the willingness of immigrants to assimilate the local way of life. Within immigrant families, there is the potential of generational tension and conflict because the second generation of immigrants, probably born outside the home country, has low emotional ties and no personal experience of living in the respective country and therefore develops a stronger attachment to the country of residence. Nevertheless, strategies differ among immigrant families and groups to nurture and maintain a strong link to the country of origin, which is easier in social structures with other compatriots (interview 2007).

For immigrants, access to the labour market is constrained. According to Portes and Sensenbrenner, many immigrants have an elite or middle class background and considerable levels of education. However, the incompatibility of degrees and diplomas with the host country's regulations limits professional opportunities, so self-employment becomes a route to upward social mobility. Self-employment enforces solidarity and bonds among immigrant families. Lower transaction cost, loyalty and interdependence favour family as business associates and employees. Bounded solidarity enforced by perceptions of a hostile environment encourages levels of interdependence and influences internal dynamics and social hierarchies (Portes and Sensenbrenner 1993:1323–1332). Nevertheless, there is a cost to solidarity in terms of constraints on personal freedom and individual development prospects because of down-levelling pressures within immigrant structures. This situation is exacerbated by conflicting value systems regarding social hierarchies, norms and validation of skills and achievements within immigrant structures when compared to mainstream society (Portes and Sensenbrenner 1993:1338–1342). Solidarity and social bonds among and within immigrant families and groups reduces ties to the host society and networks outside their immediate social structures (Lauglo 2000:166).

Moreover, discrimination and daily experiences of not belonging enforce perceptions that the stakes are higher and that professional careers and achievements are more difficult to attain as immigrants than host country citizens. Hence, schooling and education is highly valued in some immigrant communities; to overcome the challenges of a discriminating environment, immigrant children need to perform better. Education and skills development, local language proficiency and the usefulness of specific educational achievements are door openers facilitating integration and social mobility (Lauglo 2000:159–160). Immigrant communities differ regarding their validation of integration and their strategies to incorporate or separate themselves from society. A variety of coping strategies range from strong social networks that offer an alternative to host country society to the diminution of social pressure on immigrants due to distance from the home country. In particular, for immigrants coming from societies with strong traditions and rigorous hierarchies, the distance to family and society in the country of origin offers opportunities and personal development prospects away from the limitations of tradition and social control and often benefit women (Lauglo 2000:166).

The Italian and Greek immigrant communities not only have a distinct history in Johannesburg, the two respective immigrant organisations also distinguish themselves in terms of organisational structures, support by the country of origin and the facilities they offer to their communities. The result is considerable differences in terms of social bonds and identification with the home or host country. Significant groups of Italian immigrants arrived in South Africa between 1870–1920, triggered by the unification of Italy and later by World War I and the post-war period. A further wave of immigration started after World War II. Greek immigrants started coming to South Africa at the end of the 19th century. A considerable number came after World War II, mainly as a result of the Greek civil war that started during the last year of World War II and ended in 1949. The military coup in 1967 and the military dictatorship until 1974 was another reason for immigration.

The location of Orange Grove as the nearest residential area to the African Explosives and Chemical Industries in Modderfontein, which employed Italian women as mentioned in the previous chapter, was the initial reason for the Italian preference for Orange Grove. Nevertheless, the growing infrastructure of Italian shops, a theatre, a hairdresser and Papagallo, an ice cream parlour, and in particular the Italian Club were equally important factors attracting the Italian community. According to a member of the Italian community, the Italien Club was an important Italian community facility to meet people, celebrate Italian holidays and participate in sports such as soccer and boccia, a typical Italian game similar to bowls. The Catholic Church in Maryvale, close to Louis Botha Avenue and Orange Grove, was another community structure. Nuns that came mainly from Italy but also from Ireland and Bavaria lived in the building next to the church and provided an educational facility to teenage girls that fell pregnant. Nevertheless, a lot of people belonging to the Catholic Church were not members of the Italian community (interview 2008).

There is no Italian school in Johannesburg and children of Italian immigrants attend public schools. However, the Italian Embassy offers language courses. In the 1980s, the Italian Club relocated to Bedfordview. In Orange Grove there were constant problems with non-Italian residents in the club's vicinity because of the noise levels. The relocation of the club was the beginning of the end of "little Italy" in Orange Grove. Today, the Italian Consulate, still located close to Orange Grove in Houghton, and Supersconto, the Italian supermarket on Louis Botha, are two of the few remnants of the Italian community. The proficiency in Italian is another factor that contributes to the disintegration of the Italian community because children of Italians born in South Africa do not speak Italian. The Italian community still produces a weekly newspaper, but the number of subscribers is decreasing. A further facility is the Italian old age home, which is popular among the Italian settler generation but not as popular among second generation Italians. There is not a strong identification with the Italian community, and the language barrier is an obstacle. Children of Italians born in South Africa consider themselves more South African than Italian (Interview 2008).

In contrast to the Italian community, social networks are very strong within the Greek community, in fact too strong according to a member of the Greek community. The Greek community is too insular; Greeks in South Africa feel stronger bonds with Greeks in Australia than with their neighbours in the local community (interview 2007). The Greek Diaspora in South Africa provides interesting insights into the effects of government policies and the role of the state in promoting and strengthening social networks. The Greek constitution mandates support of the Greek Diaspora, and the relevant government institution is located within the Secretariat of Foreign Affairs in Greece. The World Council for Hellenes Abroad receives state funding, and it is a support structure that maintains relations both with Greek communities abroad and with the host countries. It is also involved in social support structures, education and culture. The World Council is divided into different regions; Africa and the Middle East are in the same regional structure. The Federation of Hellenic Communities and Associations of South Africa is the umbrella organisation of Greek communities in South Africa. There are geographic groups, for example Bedfordview, Houghton and Orange Grove or Pretoria, and interest groups, for example Youth, Women, and the Elderly. Activities range from cultural events and Hellenic holidays to sports and charity. Additional factors that contribute to the insularity of Greek communities are the language, Greek schools and the Orthodox Church. With the disintegration of public schools in South Africa, Greek schools become an attractive alternative, in particular for Greeks that cannot afford private education (interview 2007). Usually, the church community runs the schools and also offers Greek language courses.

According to the chairperson of Hola, the social welfare organisation of the Greek community, the Orthodox Church is of critical importance. In contrast to the Catholic Church in the Italian Community, the Greek Orthodox Church is an exclusively Greek institution. The church is also the entrance point for Greek newcomers – either new immigrants to South Africa or Greeks that move within South Africa to a new local community. Once people come to the church, they are introduced to the community and receive all the information they need regarding events and Greek facilities. The cultivation of

Greek tradition is very strong in families, even among second and third generation immigrants. The Lyceum, an international Greek organisation that promotes Greek culture, is
very active in South Africa. They are for example involved in the selection of the Chair of
Greek Language Studies at the University of Johannesburg. In addition, there is a Greek
radio station and a Greek newspaper (interview 2007).

Hola is a social support structure for people of Hellenic origin. According to the
chairperson, the Greek community seems very affluent; nevertheless, there are also very
poor individuals and families. Many Greeks live at or below the poverty line including
some old people, HIV positive people, drug addicts and incomplete families. Despite the
strong bonds within the Greek community, support structures within the Greek community are not well established. Many families are struggling themselves and have their
own problems to deal with, hence Hola is important. Hola's office is located in Norwood.
It had to be close to public transport facilities because many of the poorer community
members cannot afford a car and depend on public transport. The support provided by
Hola is an important alternative to absent social support structures of the South African
state and binds poor people closer to the Greek community. A Greek old age home is
located in Orange Grove, behind Louis Botha Avenue, and a number of Greek women
contribute with voluntary work at the institution (Interview 2007).

Conclusion – Local Communities, Social Dynamics and Politics

Local politics affects the daily lives of people in a context of conflicting interests and
power disparities. Influence and power are unevenly distributed, and social structures
differ in terms of their ability to access resources. Moreover, inequalities also affect priorities, development goals and concerns of the different population groups. Different social
organisations are very active in the two neighbourhoods and engage with local government structures, city authorities and the administration. Social relations and networks
are of critical importance to the ways these organisations work and interact. Local associations claim to represent the community based on the premise that they are open to
all newcomers willing to get involved in the community. According to this view, people
who are indifferent and uninterested in the community have themselves to blame if they
are not happy with development projects, and it is the prerogative of active community
members to decide on community affairs. In particular in more affluent communities,
the state supports these initiatives, and especially public-private partnerships are popular
because they reduce demands on state resources. Nevertheless, the state's ignorance of the
variety of population groups with different needs, demands and disparities in agency and

bargaining leverage undermines the state's efforts towards a more egalitarian society. Less powerful groups depend on public institutions that defend the public good and do not promote exclusive interests. Exclusion is based on class rather than race because development projects include property and business owners. Nevertheless, class translates into racial exclusion because, for example, most tenants in Norwood and Orange Grove are non-white.

The example of the CPF and the Residents' and Business Associations show that leadership is of critical importance, not only for the sustainability of community institutions, but also in terms of their engagement with the state and the commitment to transformation. The involvement of state institutions makes a difference, for example, the local police station and station commander critically contributed to the visibility of the CPF in the community, yet the state also limits and obstructs the role and interventions of the CPF by promoting changes to marginalise and limit the influence of the CPFs.

Safety, security, order and law enforcement influence social relations; crime has a destabilising effect on local communities and contributes to alienation between different population groups. Perceptions of crime and not actual incidents of crime inform social interactions and legitimise safety measures, irrespective of the consequences these interventions potentially have on specific population groups, for example the poor. Poverty isolates from society and inhibits political engagement. Poverty disconnects the poor from the political system because they cannot relate to the political agenda and the priorities that are promoted by dominant social groups. The development of the two neighbourhoods lacks effective poverty alleviation programmes and benefits privileged population groups. With the endorsement of the privatisation of security or the promotion of public-private partnerships the government actually undermines not only prospects of sustainable development but also its monopoly on coercion and exclusive control of the justice system.

Not only the poor but also more privileged population groups have the impression that the state does not work. The lack of accountability, the dominance of the ANC, corruption and dishonesty reduce levels of political trust and further vindicate perceptions of government inefficiency. As a result of the transition and new political hierarchies, formerly privileged population groups have reduced access to the political elite and limited influence on the state. Distrust in the state and decentralisation encourage and legitimise local mobilisation. Furthermore, the disengagement of the central state in local development initiatives, in particular in wealthier neighbourhoods, facilitates fragmentation and the promotion of particular development projects. Power shifts from the state to powerful interests and their local networks and privileges specific population groups with the necessary purchasing power. The promotion of the private sector and public-private partnerships enhances levels of control, influence and power outside the state and perceptions of government inefficiencies vindicate the legitimacy of these projects.

5 Local Schools and their Impact on Integration, Civic Engagement and Neighbourhood Sociability

Introduction

Education is a critical element in the transformation process because education is believed to empower people, enhance opportunities and increase space of agency and choice on important matters in people's lives. Furthermore, in integrated education institutions, learners from different backgrounds grow up together, develop shared interests and concerns and experience the benefits of cooperation. This environment creates important steps towards reducing inequalities, racial divisions and social boundaries. In South Africa, education was a fundamental part of oppression and played an important role in the liberation struggle. The Bantu Education Act was introduced in 1953 and constrained already limited educational opportunities even more for the black population. Education was supposed to prepare black learners for their role as labourers and servants in the economy, and it was significantly different and inferior to education for white South Africans. Schools were segregated with Bantu schools receiving substantially less financial investment and with severe limitations on educational prospects of black learners (Mungazi and Walker 1997:74–75).

Protest against the discriminatory practice of Bantu education already started in 1955 but intensified from the end of the 1960s onwards. According to Seekings, urbanisation and the increasing number of Africans born in urban areas changed demographics in cities and increased the number of Africans with access to education. The proportion of Africans born after 1950 that lived in urban areas grew from one third of the African population in 1960 to half in 1970 and two thirds in 1980. Africans growing up in urban settlements had a completely different upbringing than their parents in rural South Africa. The increase in primary and secondary education facilities expanded the access to educational opportunities from a small number of black learners to the masses. Out of this urban school-based culture, a new generation of student and youth activists emerged. The Soweto uprising in 1976 was a result of this development and a milestone in the liberation struggle (Seekings 2000:10–11). The growth of educational opportunities was therefore a factor contributing to rising political mobilisation.

On a similar note, Hall argues that the radical transformation of the British education system opened educational opportunities to less privileged population groups, contributed to a better integration of the different socio-economic classes and affected the percentage of women in secondary and tertiary institutions. The effects of educational reform were reflected in associational life and the increased number of participating women (Hall 2002:35–37). Offe and Fuchs also emphasise the effects of education on sociability for different reasons. Firstly, for an individual educational institutions are usually the first experience outside of the family. As a structure of social learning, they therefore contribute to experiences of cooperation and conflict management. Secondly, the quality and length of education correlates with socio-economic status. Finally, informal networks among peers in educational institutions are the beginning of sometimes lifelong friendships and social networks (Offe and Fuchs 2002:209).

According to Hall, the propensity of individuals to engage in the community increases with every additional year of education (Hall 2002:35–37). Similarly, Rothstein argues that people with higher levels of education or members of a higher socio-economic class tend to be more active in associational life and have more bargaining leverage (Rothstein 2002:302). Consequently, education is a critical additional intervening variable that influences social relations and increases agency and mediation skills. These are necessary requirements to select goals for collective endeavours and to organise within given opportunities and constraints of the social, economic, political and institutional context (Krishna 2002:xi, 9, 25).

Przeworski argues that lower educational achievements result in greater political scepticism and pessimism, low confidence in one's capacity to influence political decisions and only modest interest in political participation. Low levels of education rather foster indifference and rejection of democratic politics (Przeworski 1995:37). This is not the case in Southern Africa. On the contrary, according to Bratton and Mattes, it seems that higher education makes people more critical of democracy, mainly because of concerns that less educated or illiterate people might exercise their democratic rights in irresponsible or inappropriate ways. Conversely, education increases support for economic reform, and educated elites are more likely to endorse reductions in social spending. Nevertheless, education brings economic benefits and hence less dependency on the public sector (Bratton and Mattes 2004:91–92).

Education is highly valued by all population groups in South Africa and an important component of transformation, reduction of inequalities and promotion of social integration. The Reconstruction and Development Programme (RDP) highlights the important contribution of education and stipulates a single national department of education, at least ten years of compulsory education for all, a revision of educational books and resources to adapt to the values of the new South Africa, an obligation to pay special attention to the needs of less privileged groups, girls and women and provisions for further education and training, for example for people who were disadvantaged during apartheid. Moreover, the education of teachers and educators requires adaptation to the requirements of a modern economy (RDP 1994:60–67). In addition to the impact of education on civic engagement, different social structures have developed around schools, most importantly the Governing Bodies and the Parent-Teacher Associations (PTAs).

Nevertheless, the educational system is neither neutral nor immune to external influences and perpetuates inequalities, because well-informed and well-educated parents are more likely to interfere with school arrangements and increase the options of their children. Hence, the relationship between parents and the school is critically important. In contrast, less educated parents not only lack the information but also the skills to intervene and communicate with the school. They often feel intimidated and insecure in the school context. Consequently, less educated parents refrain from closer relations with the school and personal involvement despite their high expectations in the school and the benefits of education. Dynamic and assertive parents or members of school bodies such as the PTA tend to socialise in smaller, more exclusive groups. This behaviour contributes to the growing distance between educated and less educated parents, exacerbates feelings of insecurity for less educated parents and ultimately, the children in the greatest need of education are discriminated against by the system (Worms 2002:156). Similarly, Bourdieu argues that the authority of educated people, the educational system and its agents reproduces dominant classes. Without comprehensive intervention, the structural location of uneducated people renders it difficult to break through these barriers. Moreover, any modification of the educational system that would benefit less privileged learners encounters resistance and is undermined by powerful interests (Bourdieu 1998:38, Bourdieu and Passeron, 1996:5–11).

Finally, but also very importantly, local schools that are rooted in the community are institutions where children and parents from the same neighbourhood meet and become better acquainted through school projects. Schools bring people together that would otherwise not meet and serve as information facilitator in the neighbourhood beyond school programmes and events. Hence, it is interesting to investigate how the influx of new residents affects the local schools and the neighbourhood in Norwood and Orange Grove.

School Enrolment in Norwood and Orange Grove after 1994

During apartheid and racial segregation, learners were enrolled in the schools located in their neighbourhood. Schools were community structures where people from the same neighbourhood met and interacted with each other, and all came from the same racial group due to the Group Areas Act. After the Soweto Uprising and the challenges to the South African education system by black learners, Catholic schools started to defy the apartheid government and enrolled black learners. Similarly, private schools admitted black learners, mostly children of foreign diplomats and wealthy Africans. In both cases, school fees restricted access and excluded the vast majority of Africans. In the 1980s, Indian and Coloured schools started to admit black learners, and finally, white schools started to open their doors. During the transition, new registration policies allowed parents to enrol their children in schools outside of their neighbourhood to promote and encourage racial integration. After the first democratic elections in 1994, the new administration reorganised and united the two segregated departments of education into one entity. Educational reform was initiated and outlined in the *White Paper on Education and Training* in 1995 (Tihanyi 2006:51–54).

The four primary schools in the two neighbourhoods of this study are Orange Grove Primary, Norwood Primary, Houghton Primary and Paterson Park Primary. They have all been affected by the transformation in education and the changing admission policies. Primary schools include Grade 1 to Grade 7, and learners are between six or seven and twelve or thirteen years old. The four principals have all worked for a long time at their school and experienced the transition and the subsequent significant transformation of the education system. Two principals are male and two female. All are white because at the time of their respective employments, it was impossible to employ a teacher of colour in a school of a white residential area. The transformation process included different phases and policy changes, and it is complicated to get a comprehensive picture of the changes and their implications.

According to the principals, Orange Grove, Norwood and Houghton Primary Schools are classified as "Section 21" schools. Section 21 schools are administratively independent, decide on the school subjects and sports and extramural activities, appoint staff members and have a certain leverage in terms of the number of learners in each class as long as they have the necessary resources to employ additional staff. They order textbooks and stationery, and they are responsible for the maintenance of the school buildings and the payment of utility accounts. The schools also decide on school fees; this explains the differences in fees at the three public schools. Government regulations also apply to Section 21 schools, for example in terms of the admission of learners unable to afford school fees, pass rates and stipulations regarding budget allocations. Section 21 schools receive government subsidies; however, school fees, fund-raisers and business contributions are the principal sources of income (interviews 2006). In contrast, Paterson Park Primary is an independent school but subsidised by the government. It is a Seventh Day Adventist School where the curriculum is based on the religion, and teachers receive additional training after completing a public college of education qualification. The principal stated that the school is open to all interested learners; they do not have to be members of the Seventh Day Adventist Church, but they are also not exempt from religious subjects, instructions and practice. Most learners belong to the Seventh Day Adventist Church (interview 2006).

The four schools were affected by the transition in different ways. Orange Grove Primary School was a Model C school in 1990 (Model C schools were semi-private and managed by a committee and the school principal). The school was closed for one year and opened again in 1992. Today the school has 634 learners of which there are five Coloured, seven Indian and four white learners and the remaining 618 learners are African. The annual school fees are R2000 (2006). The socio-economic background of learners ranges from lower middle class to very poor, which impacts negatively on the school finances. Some learners come from the neighbourhood, mainly children of domestic staff and the police barracks. Other learners come from further away including the townships, Midrand and South Johannesburg (interview 2006).

In Norwood Primary, demographic changes started in 1994. According to the principal, Norwood Primary was an entirely white school. Not only were 80 to 90 per cent of the learners Jewish, but also a high percentage of the teaching staff were Jewish. Over a period of four years, the school lost about 150 to 200 learners every year. The composition of teachers also changed. In particular, Jewish teachers moved to private Jewish schools as there was a lot of fear regarding pensions and retirement funds in public schools after 1994. Some of the white staff members opted for retrenchment packages more for financial than political reasons, for example to pay off a home loan in an economically uncertain situation. A significant number of Jewish children also transferred to private schools. Parents value education and lost trust in the education system after 1994. The school now has 482 learners of which 18 are White, 24 Indian, 19 Coloured and 418 African. The annual school fees are R5500 (2006). Less than 20 per cent of learners live in the neighbourhood. The rest come from further away, as far away as Krugersdorp and Soweto. According to the principal, the school was approached by Angolan parents to admit ten learners from Angola. Several families are pooling resources to buy or rent a property in Norwood. Once the children are enrolled, parents will take turns in supervising the children and offer them a better education than would be possible in Angola (interview 2006).

Houghton Primary was a white Jewish school that changed in the past ten years. According to the principal, many white parents enrolled their children in private schools and affluent Indians started to move to Houghton and Norwood. Today the school has three white learners, ten Indian, 36 Coloured and 451 African learners who mainly come from further away. Only a few learners live in the neighbourhood as the school fees are less affordable for domestic staff. In 2006, the annual school fees were R6200 (interview 2006).

Paterson Park Primary, the independent Seventh Day Adventist School, already started to admit children of colour in the 1980s. According to the principal, enrolment numbers today are significantly lower than in 1994: they dropped from 175 learners in 1994 to 96 learners in 2006. In 1980, the first Coloured learners were admitted and Afrikaner parents withdrew their children. In 1986, the first black learners were admitted and "English" parents withdrew their children. Today there is one white learner left at the school, one Indian, nine Coloured and 85 African learners who come mainly from further away and not from the neighbourhood. Ten learners are not members of the Seventh Day Adventist Church of which one is a Muslim. The remaining 9 non-Adventist learners belong to different Christian churches; however, they have to attend all classes including religion. Teachers have to be members of the Seventh Day Adventist Church. There are eleven staff members, one of them male. The composition of staff is a "good racial mixture" according to the principal. There is a registration fee of R500 and eleven payments of R835, amounting to annual school fees of R9685 (2006).

Consequences of Changing Admission Policies

The changing demographics of learners and the extended catchment area of the four schools included in this study had far-reaching consequences. Transport is an ongoing problem in all schools; learners coming from the townships, Midrand, the south of Johannesburg or even further away mainly depend on public transport. According to all principals, transport is unreliable and there is only limited transport during strikes, so frequently children arrive late and the latecomers disrupt classes (interviews 2006). It is an ongoing process to stress that learners have to be on time and this has to be enforced in the interest of those learners arriving on time and to prevent the problem from getting worse. A further problem is that some learners have to wait for their parents to fetch them until five or six o'clock in the afternoon during the week. If parents do not have the money for aftercare, they tell their children to walk around, for example along Grant Avenue, and come back to the school premises at six o'clock. There were parents suggesting that their children stay overnight with the cleaners or the gardener living on the school property, which cannot be allowed. The distance between school and home also influences social relations among learners. Most children live in different parts of Johannesburg, hence they are not able to socialise with each other due to organisational and transport problems. Occasional visits to friends from the school have to be arranged in advance; transport problems inhibit any spontaneity and deprive children of important social experiences, constraining the development of social competence (interviews 2006).

The distance between home and school also affects parental engagement. Many parents are not involved in school activities, so there are problems finding parents to volunteer for the PTA, stand for election into the Governing Body or help with extramural activities, tuck shops and fund-raisers. In addition, parents barely know each other and do not seem interested in more personal relations with other families. The distance between home and school and the cost of transport are a deterrent, and many parents do not attend parents' evenings or report card discussions. They neither help with the organisation of fund-raisers and sports events nor attend these events (interviews 2006).

Changes in the Learning and Social Environment

The four principals are challenged by the changing school policies and regulations. The consequences are manifold and affect schools, teachers and learners in different ways. The four principals consider it more demanding, stressful and difficult to be a teacher and educator today. Stress levels, tensions, pressures and emotional strains are considerable, but most of the problems are not related to teaching but to the social and institutional environment, the family context of learners and the school's financial situation. It is demanding every day to cope with the various problems and troubles, yet there is barely any support structure from the provincial administration or the Department of Education. According to the principals, being a teacher is much more work than it used to be, and yet one has the impression of not achieving anything – the problems are never-ending. The school environment has changed completely in the past ten years and principals also have to care about the well-being of the teachers at their school, who are struggling with stress, nervous tensions and emotional pressures. There are high levels of commitment and dedication; teachers try their best, but burnouts and exhaustion affect levels of motivation and a number of teachers would choose a different career today. It is a problem that most of the white parents have taken their children out of the schools, and the principals were neither prepared for nor imagined the social problems they confront today (interviews 2006).

In all four schools, subjects are taught in English; however, there are significant differences in proficiency when learners start their school education. Orange Grove and

Norwood Primary have "grannies" from the neighbourhood to help with the readings; this is one of the few neighbourhood structures that has survived. Many learners develop a nice relationship with the grannies and are fond of them, so it is a valuable support structure. Pass rates are an additional problem because they are prescribed by the Ministry of Education, and schools are only allowed to fail five per cent of learners, the rest has to pass. Sometimes it would make more sense for the learner to repeat a year and have more time to improve skills; the learners that have to be passed will struggle for the rest of their education. An additional year of schooling for struggling learners is not discrimination but an opportunity time to catch up with deficits. There are no support structures to address the immense structural dissimilarities between children when they start school. Some children were in preschools and come well prepared, in contrast to children from disadvantaged backgrounds that barely speak English (interviews 2006).

Intergroup dynamics, gender relations and conflict resolution strategies are influenced by the social environment and its hierarchies at the homes of learners. In many cases children experience the use of violence as a means of addressing and resolving disputes and conflict. Even young boys sometimes feel privileged as males and superior to girls, so they hassle or tease girls. There is also bullying of younger learners by older ones. The schools invest a great deal of time and effort into social interactions, problem solving, conflict resolution and the empowerment of girls and younger children. Various support structures are involved in these programmes. In most cases, there is little support from parents for these programmes because they are in conflict with the parents' understanding of the social order (interviews 2006).

A certain degree of conflict or fighting is normal, but there are limits, and the school has to act when learners are insulting or cruel to others. The language of some learners and the name-calling can be very offensive. The older the boys are, the more difficult it becomes to prevent teasing, bullying and insulting of girls and the use of explicitly sexually discriminatory language. Ethnicity and to a lesser degree race are an issue, mostly between Africans because in all schools the vast majority of learners is black. For example, a few African parents did not want their children to learn Zulu. A number of African parents also have a problem with African teachers: the reputation of township schools is bad, and this is the reason why parents prefer schools outside the townships, despite transport problems. In one of the schools, parents were unhappy when the school started to employ Indian teachers. However, school policy regarding appointments is not based on affirmative action but on the selection of the best qualified teacher. There was an incidence of xenophobia at one of the schools and the principal explains that the tea lady was on maternity leave, and so she employed an Angolan woman as replacement – the unemployed and destitute mother of a learner. It caused a huge problem: many parents and employees, for example the cleaners, verbally attacked the principal for giving the job to a foreigner and not employing a South African. It was so bad that the school would never consider employing a foreigner again, just because it resulted in too many problems in circumstances that are already difficult enough (interviews 2006).

Crime is a problem. All schools have been affected and security measures are an additional cost factor, for example a guard at the gate. Norwood Police Station is in contact with the schools, and they offer an "Adopt a Cop" programme that is used by all four schools. The same police officer visits the school regularly and develops a relationship with the learners. The police officer provides useful information ranging from problems around traffic to conflict resolution, how to protect oneself and available support structures in times of crisis. The "school cop" is also involved in cases of abuse, opens dockets and initiates investigations. All schools have problems with petty theft; there are strategies to prevent theft, for example to ask parents to transfer money directly into the school account instead of sending it with their child. In more serious cases, the "school cop" is called in (interview 2006).

The four schools are affected by the HIV/AIDS crisis. The schools promote the policy that everybody has to be careful and act as if everyone is infected with the virus because the HIV status of learners is not always known. In Orange Grove Primary, a considerable number of learners have already lost one or both parents: out of 634 learners, ten are orphaned, 22 have lost their mother and 57 have lost their father. In most cases, the cause of death is not revealed. In addition, many learners lose relatives and are often at funerals over the weekend. Witnessing the illness and death of a parent is a traumatic experience, but often the school is not informed about what is happening at home. In particular, younger learners often do not know or realise what causes the illness of the parent. The stigma attached to HIV/AIDS prevents older children from talking about it or seeking help (interviews 2006).

Abuse is another problem, and in all four schools interventions were necessary. Some learners were severely beaten, there were a few incidents of rape and there is also psychological abuse. Learners are afraid to speak to an adult about their experiences because they have the impression that they misbehaved and deserved this treatment. It is a dilemma how far schools can go to discuss problems and shortcomings with parents because, instead of supporting and helping their children, parents possibly resort to beatings. It sometimes takes a while until a teacher can ascertain what is wrong, for example with a difficult, disruptive or introverted learner. There was a case of a boy whose parents are refugees. The learner was severely abused at home, Childline was called, but it was also a traumatic experience for the principal due to the severity of the abuse. The Psychology Department of the University of the Witwatersrand provides support structures to Orange Grove Primary and Paterson Park Primary, in addition to Childline, the social welfare department and victim support structures. All principals state that it is important that the school acts on these problems, but it is additional work, a psychological stress and emotional strain. In certain instances when the school was addressing the abuse of children, parents and the child in question disappeared. Life skills development programmes are offered in all schools, and they include the problem of violence and abuse, and information on victim support structures (interviews 2006).

School Finances and Governmental Support Structures

All four schools have financial problems. Government policies waiving school fees for poor parents are a huge problem. Poor parents do not have to pay school fees, but government subsidies are way below the cost of the fees. The campaigns of the government, the ANC and its allies that exempt poor people from school fees do not disclose how insufficient government subsidies are. Hence, government subsidies are not a substitute for the lacking parental contributions, which exacerbates the financial crisis at public schools. According to one principal, many parents could at least contribute something – maybe not the full amount but just something – but they think they do not have to pay at all. In 2006, only 33 per cent of parents paid school fees at Orange Grove Primary. The school is financially not viable, and at the moment, the school has a massive cash flow problem. School finances also limit extramural activities because of transport costs, for example sports events with other schools or excursions (interviews 2006).

Norwood and Houghton Primary have smaller classes of only twenty instead of forty learners per class. According to the two principals, the government calculates the number of teachers based on forty learners per class and pays those teachers' salaries; additional teachers are the financial responsibility of the school. School fees in both schools are higher than at Orange Grove Primary. The smaller classes make the schools attractive to the middle class, but the schools have already admitted a few learners that are only able to pay part of the school fees. Because the schools can afford smaller classes, the government can compel them to admit more learners. Both principals are worried that once the number of learners from destitute parents increases and the schools lack the resources to keep classes smaller, the middle class will withdraw their children. It is not the case that wealthier parents in wealthier suburbs subsidise poor children because the lacking resources of public schools are one of the reasons why wealthier parents prefer private schools for their children's education. Another reason why public schools are unattractive is the social problems of children coming from a disadvantaged background because they affect the learning environment. Wealthier parents are concerned with the quality of education and can opt for private schools if standards at public schools are below their expectations (interviews 2006).

Government subsidies and financial contributions are insufficient. It is easy to waive school fees and then delegate the problems arising from this policy to the individual schools. The four principals have the impression that the government assumes schools in wealthier suburbs have ample resources at their disposal. Despite interventions, the government refuses to see the reality. Decreasing school resources are not only the result of declining parental contributions, there is also less funding from businesses in the area and lacking parental support for fund-raisers. The denial of problems by government structures has far-reaching consequences and not only affects the financial viability of schools. There are no institutionalised support structures or counselling for teachers, despite the difficult social environment of schools with the levels of stress and emotional pressure emanating from it. Lacking support structures and the passing on of problems to the schools, for example regarding school fees or pass rates, create the impression that the schools are unable to deal with these challenges. This process undermines the authority of principals and teachers and the cooperation between parents and the schools (interviews 2006).

Many government policies and regulations are imposed without prior consultation since not everyone would agree to these measures. In contrast to administrators, consultants or politicians, teachers can sometimes see the potential problems of policies. The government is unapproachable and sometimes quite arrogant, frequently relating concerns or criticism to questions of race and discrimination without even considering thinking about the problems. After the implementation of certain regulations or policies, there is no evaluation or discussion of the merits and problems arising from them, which would be critical to make adjustments and reconsider questionable outcomes. The vast majority of school surveys focus on equity, but there are other areas in dire need of attention. The prescribed pass rates are not in the interest of learners from disadvantaged backgrounds. It would be urgent to provide support structures for learners with difficulties instead of insinuating that the schools are discriminating against poorly performing learners from disadvantaged backgrounds, thereby discrediting the respective teacher or school. For example, the opportunity to attend nursery school would prepare disadvantaged children better and make a difference once they start school. The education system does not address the structural differences of learners when they start their schooling. Even in a context of equal opportunities, these structural disparities disadvantage less privileged learners from the beginning of their school careers. Ultimately it does not directly affect either the principal or the teachers if they let a learner pass against their better judgement. Usually that learner has even more problems in the next grade: the less a learner understands, the harder it is for him or her to follow and keep up with the class programme. Indeed, the high pass rates contribute to dropping school standards, which impacts on the reputation of public schools. Under these circumstances, the middle class, irrespective of race opts for private schools (interviews 2006).

Better support and communication structures would allow schools to recognise problems at an earlier stage and to consider appropriate interventions. The principals are concerned about cooperation with government structures. The inadequate levels of communication result in problems that the schools did not create but have to address. Teachers feel powerless in the face of changes they cannot control, and subsequent problems increase the daily work load, contribute to high levels of stress and generate feelings of isolation and resentment. Moreover, the inadequate communication between the schools and government institutions sets a bad example for the communication and cooperation between schools and parents (interviews 2006).

Education and Transformation – Schools in Norwood and Orange Grove

Education is highly valued in post-apartheid South Africa, and parents of all socio-economic classes and varying levels of education select the schools for their children. For example, parents living in townships enrol their children in public schools in formerly white residential areas, or Muslim parents enrol their children in a Christian independent school despite organisational problems and additional transport costs. Parents are concerned with the education of their children. This fact stands in contrast to the importance parents assign to communication and cooperation with the school. Besides the distance between the homes of learners and the school, there is also no tradition of parental school involvement. For a number of parents, school experiences were shaped and hierarchically controlled by the apartheid state, so they never had the opportunity to experience the benefits of cooperation between teachers and parents. Hence, the question arises whether lacking parental involvement is only a question of distance and transport costs or also a question of conflicting values regarding the necessity of parental engagement or of social class. According to different interviewees, in contrast to public schools, parental engagement in private schools is high.

In the context of the South African transition and the legacies of apartheid, education, integration and the elimination of discrimination and inequalities are critical objectives. Admission policies at schools were well intended measures to reverse these problems. Considering the outcome today, it is necessary to admit that these policy changes resulted in unexpected consequences and were ultimately counterproductive. Wealthier middle class parents able to afford more expensive schools have left public schools in their neighbourhood. Affluent Indians moving into the area also send their children to private schools. In contrast to the annual fees of the four schools included in this study that ranged from R2000 to R9700, the annual cost of more expensive schools varies between R17000 to R20000. Parents with the necessary financial means select schools with a better reputation; the cost factor and transport problems matter less than the quality of education. Race is not the problem because private schools are racially integrated. The lacking school resources and above all the social problems in public schools are a deterrent. Socio-economic class rather than race is the determinant in school choices; however, given the history of inequality and racial discrimination, the majority of lower class people are black and thus class translates into race. The crisis in public schools has detrimental consequences not only for the individual learner but also on levels of skills development with their economic and political consequences. The crisis is exacerbated by the critical role education plays in addressing the multiple problems of inequality and the impact education has on citizenship and propensity for civic engagement. The withdrawal of the middle class from public schools not only increases inequalities but also removes an important structure from public schools capable of exerting pressure on government institutions.

Schools with a large catchment area are less embedded in the neighbourhood, which impacts on supportive social structures and neighbourhood sociability. Schools are not community structures any more and are neither embedded nor engaged with the neighbourhood. Schools used to contribute to fund-raisers in the neighbourhood, were part of social life and were involved in community structures, for example the library or the old age home. Schools enabled parents to build mutual support structures, for example for aftercare or for help in emergencies. People that know each other are more likely to be aware of a person or family in trouble, which allows assistance or intervention with preventive measures. In the current situation, the teachers frequently neither know the locality nor living conditions of learners and their families. It is possible that teachers are not told of a parent dying of HIV/AIDS, even though a better knowledge of a learner's social environment would help to provide support structures. In case of disputes or conflict, parents can withdraw their child and practically disappear, for example if legal procedures are imminent as a consequence of child abuse (interviews 2006).

Families not living in the neighbourhood do not use the local infrastructure, for example the library, shops and businesses. Fund-raisers are much easier to organise by local people who use local shops and businesses. Residents can approach local shops and stand a better chance as customers to receive donations and contributions, or they can even offer an invitation to shops or businesses to attend the event. The business community has less incentive to contribute to schools where parents are not potential customers because they live and shop elsewhere. Schools rooted in the neighbourhood provide information structures among community members, either through personal contacts or through the information boards at schools. Not only schools but also individual community members and groups can use these information channels to disseminate information, from useful contacts to community services and upcoming events. Schools that are embedded in the neighbourhood contribute to the strengthening of relations and a sense of community. Cooperation is facilitated in communities where people know each other because information and organisational arrangements are necessary to deal with community affairs, tackle problems and mobilise people around collective demands or grievances. Structures of social control work better and have an effect on responsible behaviour and levels of respect in communities where people know each other.

Finally, community structures around schools offer important social experiences to learners that influence and shape socialisation structures and affect levels of social competence. In schools that are not rooted in the community, children are not able to socialise in the neighbourhood because their friends live elsewhere. Children depend on transport to socialise with their friends or to engage in sports and other activities. This situation affects the scope of decisions, the level of independence and the spontaneity of children and teenagers because social contacts need to be planned in advance and depend on the parents' willingness to provide transport. These restrictions deprive children and teenagers of important social experiences by limiting the independence to manage their own personal relations.

To conclude, the implications of school and admission policy adjustments that intended to facilitate racial integration and increase access to educational opportunities for disadvantaged population groups have far-reaching consequences on sociability, quality of education and propensity of social engagement. Social structures are affected in two ways: firstly, there are changes in the school as learner demographics have completely changed, and contacts and social interactions between teachers and parents and between the school and government institutions are in many cases minimal. Secondly, there are changes in the neighbourhoods around schools because there is no interest in local affairs from people that do not live in the community. Schools therefore contribute less to social institutions in the neighbourhood and to community life. Moreover, the quality of education in public schools has dropped, but wealthier parents can afford alternatives. In contrast, less privileged and less educated parents have to put up with public schools and are not in a position to exert pressure on the government and demand quality education for their children.

6 Religious Communities and Responses to the Challenges of Transformation, Value Changes and Inequality

Introduction

Institutions of faith encourage social relations and social engagement and in South Africa, a number of institutions of faith were involved in the liberation struggle and the democratisation process. Today, prominent clerics voice their opinion on contemporary problems and challenges. Institutions of faith are important social structures in post-apartheid South Africa: they emphasise the importance of community and social values such as solidarity, compassion and social cohesion and influence the quality of social relations. Institutions of faith open spaces where the different population groups can meet. Institutions of faith engage with the changing social and political environment, offer guidance and influence the nature of social interactions and relations with their moral standards. Institutions of faith differ in terms of their engagement and integration in society. As the most prominent civil society structure in South Africa, institutions of faith contribute to the vibrancy of associational life.

Institutions of faith shape moral values and offer spiritual guidance. Nevertheless, the growing secularisation of society and emphasis on personal responsibility resulted in more scepticism, increasing rejection of religious prescriptions and movement away from the hierarchical structure and dominance of religious institutions. Society's more secular orientation and the values promoted by the South African transition did not result in a decline or disappearance of moral values and ethical standards. On the contrary, new values emanating from liberalism and personal responsibility promote democratic and civil liberties, cultural diversity, solidarity, human rights and respect for the environment. As a result, membership in religious institutions has become more polarised and has, for example, declined in liberal Christian denominations but increased in conservative and fundamentalist religious institutions (Egan 2007:451). Hence, institutions of faith can develop into distinct and exclusive social structures that provide an alternative to secular societies through their adherence to conservative or fundamentalist moral values.

Family tradition and socialisation are essential factors determining religious affiliation in South Africa. Even today, interfaith marriages can be a challenge for individual families. People do not mind if members of the community have a partner from another denomination but are more hesitant to confront their own family with a partner from a different faith group. The different Christian denominations do not actively recruit new members but rather encourage their members to approach potential newcomers. They open their doors to any person interested in joining provided they adhere to the Christian faith. In some denominations, membership is confirmed by baptism. The Jewish community is reluctant to accept people converting to Judaism. New members, for example as a result of an inter-faith marriage, participate in the community for a certain time before they are allowed to become full members. In the case of a family with only one Jewish parent and one from another religion, children only become members of the Jewish community by birth if the mother is Jewish, since mothers are more important in religious education. The Muslim community has no problem with people converting to Islam as long as they are willing to follow the Quran (interviews 2006, 2007). Buildings of institutions of faith are visible structures in communities. It is easy for newcomers to find them, for example in comparison to residents' association without a permanent office space.

Institutions of faith have existed over centuries and survived fundamental changes and times of crises, so they value their long-standing beliefs, traditions, ethical standards and moral values. Nevertheless, religious institutions are affected by history, transformation and development. They have to engage and cope with a changing socio-cultural and political environment. It can also be a challenge to make the religious community attractive to the younger generation. In contrast, the older generation has difficulty adapting to changes. In liberal denominations, levels of conflict are low as people tend to rather leave the church than to debate and confront contentious issues (interviews 2006, 2007).

Religious institutions are characterised by trust, norms of reciprocity and structures of social control; the degree of social cohesion varies as well as the nature of relations with society. Social control provides a sense of stability, but it is not only a positive quality of social structures because networks and their measures of control also potentially constrain individual agency. Group solidarity, conformity and shared norms and values possibly exert downward levelling pressure on members (Portes and Landolt 1996:41). There is little space for new ideas or initiatives from members, particularly if they are young (Worms 2001:141). Moreover, institutions of faith have an ambiguous relationship to trust because religious values potentially contribute to insulation from mainstream society and from disbelievers. Hence, strong social bonds that increase levels of trust are possibly enforced through the promotion of a suspicious attitude towards outsiders or used for selfish and anti-social purposes. According to Foley, Edwards, Portes and Uslaner, insulation encourages antagonism towards other groups, and race is one of the most powerful determinants of particularised trust in religious institutions (Foley and Edwards 1999:155, Portes 1998:17, Uslaner 2002:87–88, 107). Religious organisations bring people together; participation not only develops citizenship skills but also satisfies needs for belonging (Berman 1997:404). The sense of belonging through shared norms and values can provide a moral sanctuary in a rapidly changing environment. Nevertheless, the symbolic membership in "imagined communities" can also trigger powerful and potentially destructive emotions from the strong identification with the religious community (Whiteley 1999:29–31). Institutions of faith are not socially or politically neutral. Civic engagement is not a side effect of religious practice; on the contrary, institutions of faith have their own agenda, specific concerns and distinct aspirations (Fried 2002:36).

Bourdieu argues that any form of tradition, not just religion, influences socialisation and education, contributing to the perpetuation of social hierarchies and privileges (Bourdieu 1996:5–10, 1998:37–38). Hence, norms and values emanating from hierarchical structures of authority in religious or traditional institutions are passed down from generation to generation through socialisation. They are inculcated and adopted for non-rational reasons such as faith and feelings of duty. In contrast, the adoption of liberal values occurs in a context of critical engagement and space of debate (McLean et al. 2002:10). Usually, clerics are in a position of authority. Their values and ethical standards influence social life in their community and the degree of engagement or withdrawal from society. Many institutions of faith generate their own resources and this financial independence offers options of disengagement from society.

Religion and Society in South Africa

Religion, immigration and colonisation are historically linked in South Africa. Missionaries from different Christian denominations, Dutch and British colonists, Malay slaves, Indian indentured workers and Jewish immigrants all brought their religions to South Africa. They marginalised and replaced indigenous religions and contributed to the diversity of South Africa's religious life. Christians, Muslims and Jews are included in this study because the three religions are represented in Norwood and Orange Grove. According to the 2001 census, 78.8 per cent of the South African population belong to a Christian denomination, the largest religious group. Of this number, 32.6 per cent of South Africans belong to an African Initiated Church in comparison to 16.5 per cent Protestants, 7.2 per cent Dutch Reformed Church members, 7.1 per cent Catholics and 5.9 per cent members of a Pentecostal Church. In all Christian denominations, membership has decreased between the 1996 and the 2001 census except for the African Initiated Churches: the percentage of the population belonging to an African Initiated Church increased from 26.3 to 32.6 per cent (quoted in Egan 2007:451). According to the 2001 census, 1.5 per cent of the population are Muslim and 0.2 per cent are Jewish (Census 2001).

The overall racial composition of Christians reflects the demographic composition of the population. However, the racial composition varies significantly between the different Christian denominations. Indians and Coloureds comprise approximately 87.3 per cent of Muslims, Blacks comprise 11.4 per cent and Whites about 1.3 per cent. In the Jewish community, approximately 82 per cent of members are white, 15.8 per cent are black and 0.8 per cent are Indian or coloured (Census 2001). Religion is important in South Africa: 43 per cent of the population are members of a religious institution. This percentage is the highest proportion of group membership when compared to other civil society organisations, such as the less than 20 per cent of the population that are members of a political party, which is the second largest proportion of membership in civil society structures (wa Kivilu 2002:125). Membership figures of religious institutions neither correlate with engagement in the religious community nor the attendance of services. They also do not reveal the gender composition and age structure of active and passive members of particular institutions.

South Africa never had a state religion, but the influence of Christianity dominates in comparison to other religions. Despite the secular state and the promotion of diversity, national holidays commemorating significant events in South Africa's history are supplemented with additional public holidays for important Christian religious celebrations. Nevertheless, the constitutional right to freedom of religion allows members of any religious community to celebrate their religious holy days irrespective of work commitments and obligations. The Dutch Reformed Church (DRC) was historically close to the state, and its authority increased during the apartheid years. The DRC was a central pillar of Afrikaner community and shaped Afrikaner identity. Moreover, the DRC provided a social security net to impoverished Afrikaners. The DRC not only influenced the moral order, dominant values and Afrikaner identity, it also provided a justification for racial discrimination. Together with the Afrikaner Broederbond, a secret organisation restricted to carefully selected Protestant white men, the DRC not only cooperated with the apartheid state but a number of its clerics were also incumbents in political office and members of the Broederbond (Beinart 1994:155–116). Nevertheless, a number of dissident clerics of the DRC criticised and attacked the apartheid system, contesting interpretations of the Bible that served to justify racial discrimination.

The democratisation and secularisation of the state together with the promotion of more liberal values diminished the influence the DRC and Christian churches in general had on politics and society. The liberalisation of abortion, legalisation of homosexuality, secularisation of education and promotion of tolerance shaped new values and influenced perceptions of decency, acceptable behaviour and moral standards in personal relations, culture, the arts and public life (Egan 2007:448–450). Institutions of faith responded in various ways to apartheid and the transition to democracy. They ranged from condemnation of racism to providing the ideological underpinning of apartheid. Changes as a result of the transition affect intergenerational relations within specific religious groups and influence responses to the challenges of inequality, the consequences of racial discrimination, the high levels of crime and violence and the HIV/AIDS crisis. The secularisation of the state and the promotion of liberal values is reflected in democratic and civil liberties, gender equality, cultural diversity, human rights and respect for the environment. These social values potentially conflict with values cherished by institutions of faith, for example the perception of gender roles within the hierarchical, patriarchal structures of religious institutions. The various institutions of faith employ different strategies to engage with the challenges of value changes and the new societal order.

All institutions of faith included in this study depend entirely on contributions from their members and additional income generated by letting out facilities. In some institutions, members are encouraged to commit to monthly contributions to allow better planning and budgeting. All Christian Churches in wealthier suburbs have to support church communities in townships or impoverished areas. In general, donations are voluntary and at the discretion of individual contributors. As several clerics pointed out, ultimately donations are a private matter between the individual and the Creator, and people have to decide how much the institution is worth to them. However, especially in smaller communities, measures of social control enforce financial commitments and obligations to a certain extent. In some of the Christian churches, interview partners pointed at the situation of African community members who already have considerable financial obligations towards family members not living in the same household. This situation limits their financial abilities and hence contributions to the church. In most cases, clerics respect the different loyalties of church members and acknowledge that these people are willing to share their resources with others. Nevertheless, community members do sometimes have the impression that black congregation members do not honour their obligations of supporting the church, which is a potential source of conflict (interviews 2006).

Institutions of Faith and Heterogeneity in Norwood and Orange Grove

Levels of racial integration differ in the various religious communities in Norwood and Orange Grove. Heterogeneity is not only affected by changing demographics and the influx of different population groups. A considerable number of domestic workers living in the area are also members of one of the Christian churches. During apartheid, special services were offered to them in English and indigenous languages, a practice that continues in some churches today. This practice contributes to the fragmentation of the community; nevertheless, divisions are more along class than racial lines because the African middle class attends church services in English. In the two Jewish communities members are mainly white, despite the fact that only 82 per cent of the South African Jews are white according to the 2001 Census. The Muslim community is relatively new in the area – a consequence of the influx from Lenasia and Mayfair in the second half of the 1990s. There is a provisional prayer facility and a mosque is under construction.

The Christian Churches included in this study are the Anglican Churches of St. Augustine and St. Luke, The Methodist Churches in Berea, Aldersgate and Forest Town, the Le Roux and Lyndhurst Baptist Churches, the Dutch Reformed Church in Orchards, the Presbyterian Church in Orchards and the Maryvale Catholic Church. Two of the clerics interviewed are African, one is female. Furthermore, representatives of the Jewish and Muslim communities and from the Caring Women's Forum, a Muslim charity, were included.

The Challenges of Racial, Gender and Socio-Economic Inequalities

The various Christian denominations have reacted in different ways to apartheid and racial segregation. Today, all denominations condemn racial discrimination. In the Jewish community with a strong family tradition and the passing on of religious practice from one generation to the other, race was never a central issue within the community. There are only a few non-white members: These mainly stem from inter-faith marriages, but there are also black members from the Jewish communities from the horn of Africa, for example the Falasha in Ethiopia. Considering the history of persecution of Jews, Judaism condemns any form of racism, and a number of Jews were active in the liberation struggle in South Africa (interviews 2007). In contrast to the Jewish and Christian community, the Muslim community was affected by racial discrimination. The end of apartheid has increased opportunities and choices; however, the Muslim community has a number of less privileged and impoverished members, a legacy of apartheid.

In Christian churches, the racial composition of the community has changed, and the racial composition also varies between different services at the same church and between different Christian denominations. In terms of racial differences at specific services, interview partners emphasised that class and not race is the decisive denominator. Domestic workers living in the area like attending services in indigenous languages with more singing and dancing; in contrast, the "middle class services" are racially mixed. It seems that style is more important than language, and a number of people prefer services with singing and music. Because of the increasing number of immigrants, it is more difficult to have services in one indigenous language. In both Baptist Churches, there are no services in indigenous languages in order to unify the community; it was a conscious decision to end the practice of different language services in order to promote integration (interviews 2006, 2007). The accommodation of diversity can become a challenge. Xenophobia is a problem, in particular among people in a difficult and uncertain economic situation. People commonly resort to stereotypical views that foreigners steal jobs, wives and girl-friends. Especially in areas with a high number of unemployed people, tensions between the different population groups increase and xenophobia becomes more salient. Religion is a common denominator, yet it seems that members of the same congregation differ in terms of interaction and integration with fellow members, in particular those coming from different socio-cultural or racial groups. Religion does not unite beyond identity.

Institutions of faith promote the equality of all human beings. This ideology is in stark contrast to the hierarchical structure and dominant role of men in religious institutions. All institutions of faith included in this study assign particular attributes, duties and obligations to members that differ significantly between men and women. Even in more gender conscious churches, daily practices, habits and sometimes the language operate against women. Organisational structures are dominated by men, and in many institu-tions of faith, certain positions are the prerogative of men. In addition, social practice discriminates against women. Even if a post is open for women, selection procedures are more stringent and female clerics are more critically monitored than it would be the case with a male cleric (interviews with 2006, 2007).

In Muslim and Jewish communities, women are excluded from religious office, and often sons have a specific position within family hierarchies. Jewish mothers are entrusted with the religious aspects of education and the upholding and safeguarding of the Jew-ish tradition, which is important in the Diaspora. The Muslim Community stresses the important position of women in Muslim families. A Muslim interview partner argued that women have a high status in society, which is the reason why they do not have to work. Women deserve that someone takes care of them. In addition, as this interview partner argued, 98 per cent of Muslim women wearing a veil do so out of choice and not coercion (interviews with 2006, 2007). A female interview partner stated that all women participating in the Caring Women's Forum have university degrees and have chosen to be mothers and stay at home in order to look after their families (interview 2006).

In institutions of faith, moral and social values are more important than materialistic achievements. Hence, moral obligations towards less fortunate people are stressed, and volunteering in favour of the poor and destitute is encouraged. Institutions of faith are the main contributors to charity and volunteer programmes (Wuthnow 2002:65). Nevertheless, many approaches to civic engagement disregard inequalities that are based on patriarchy, tradition, religion, ethnicity or class and affect the position of women (Mohan 2001:157). Charity work is mainly the domain of women because civil society structures are not autonomous but permeated by particular interests and patronage. Despite the promotion of human rights and gender equality, which should therefore also inform social practice, these values are often in conflict with traditional structures at the local level (Molyneux 2002:176). Within the hierarchical, patriarchal structures of religious institutions, dominant perceptions of gender roles not only acknowledge the important contribution of women to communities and the social fabric. They also perpetuate assumptions that women are naturally less self-interested, more altruistic and more inclined to serve their families and communities as linked to their responsibilities and role in reproduction. The assumption that women are available and do not mind unpaid work, together with moral obligations and measures of social control, potentially contribute to a substantial increase in the workload of women without any prospects of remuneration or skills development opportunities and produce considerable but unacknowledged costs for women (Molyneux 2002:178–179).

In all religious communities included in this study, only women are actively involved in charity programmes; men contribute to charity with financial donations. In addition, volunteering women are mostly white, middle class and over thirty, frequently over forty years old. It seems that mothers become involved in the community once their children grow older. In contrast to institutions of faith, in Lifeline for example, the crisis counselling centre in Norwood, demographics of volunteers have moved away from older, white middle class women. The number of younger people professionally interested in counselling as a supplement to their education is increasing, and the number of men is growing in this group. However, the centre needs more volunteers that speak African languages (interviews 2006).

Christian communities are less discriminating to non-members in connection with providing charity than the Muslim and Jewish communities. The local synagogue's charity goes only to needy Jewish families; there is a strong feeling of belonging within this community. The regional and national structures of the synagogues are involved in charity and educational work that is not entirely focused on the Jewish community (interview 2007). The Caring Women's Forum benefits not only the Muslim community; however, certain donors explicitly specify the beneficiaries of their contributions, and there is a strong sense of belonging within the Muslim community. Often for the Zakaat, donors explicitly only want to benefit needy Muslims. The Zakaat is one of the five pillars of Islam: it stipulates the duty to share resources with the less fortunate. The Forum has a separate bank account for this fund (interview 2006).

Charity programmes of the various Christian denominations differ depending on the location of the religious institution, the contacts of clerics or congregation members, financial resources and the number of people willing to engage in the programmes. However, there are also common characteristics to charity work, for example the asymmetrical relationship between the donor and the recipient. There are often criteria to distinguish between people that are worthy and those that are unworthy of charity, which are linked to perceptions of what constitutes a good and decent person, and there are expectations regarding gratitude or reciprocity, for example attendance at church services. Unfulfilled expectations can burden relations and contribute to conflict and discrimination. Moreover, as one cleric argues, even if people are involved in charity, they are far removed from social realities in Johannesburg and the consequences of apartheid and the Group Areas Act. White people are not aware of what happens in poor areas. Today's residential arrangements prevent the middle class from coming across poor locations in the city, so people have no idea about the extent of poverty and consider Johannesburg a wealthy city (interviews 2006, 2007).

Sennett differentiates between compassion for the poor aimed at feeling good and compassion aimed at doing good (Sennett 2003:128). In different denominations, single mothers are considered a problem, and they are blamed for their irresponsible behaviour; donors stress that they only receive support because it is not the child's fault. Any incidents of additional pregnancies out of wedlock result in a humiliating degree of stigmatisation and condemnation (interviews 2006, 2007). Teenage pregnancy is a problem at different churches. Teenaged mothers and pregnant teenagers receive support; however, it is a process of overcoming prejudices of other congregation members. The number of young, black, single mothers is much higher than in other racial groups. Some of the churches also help to reintegrate these young mothers back into school after the birth of their babies. A number of these women often marry years later, and not the father of their first child. Some of the clerics argued that it is surprising how willingly these men accept responsibility for the first child although it is not their own (interviews 2006, 2007).

Poor people depend on the consistency of charity services, which sometimes exceeds the capacity of voluntary organisations. Some churches provide meals or food parcels, even twice a week for homeless or poor people in the area. There are a few white people in this group of destitute recipients. Other volunteer programmes are involved in different activities around HIV/AIDS, for example information for domestic workers living with

HIV/AIDS, the training of people caring for AIDS patients, and a support group for people living with HIV/AIDS, or there are support structures to child-headed households and poor families affected by AIDS (interview 2006). Molyneux argues that even though charity and moral obligations towards the poor are an important aspect of religious practice, citizens' involvement in charity reduce the state's burden, move away from contested issues such as citizenship rights and social inclusion and rarely confront the roots of social inequalities (Molyneux 2002:174–176). Charity not only acquits the state of duties and responsibilities towards impoverished citizens, it also takes place in a context of highly unequal power relations that sometimes purposely or unintentionally generates humiliating dependencies.

Engagement with Questions of Reconciliation, Complicity and Guilt

The legacies of apartheid, traumatic experiences of discrimination and the structural differences between beneficiaries and victims of apartheid continue to affect South African inter-racial relations. The question arises of how institutions of faith address the contentious issue of conformity and guilt, and the question of reconciliation considering the commitment to moral values and compassion. Compensation and restitution for apartheid victims is marginalised in public debate and only promoted by a number of non-governmental and advocacy groups: organisations that consider compensations a moral obligation for beneficiaries of apartheid. The majority of interview partners from Christian Churches were disappointingly vague and evasive, denying any complicity or guilt. Generally, clerics emphasised that they never endorsed apartheid but also were not in a position to defy it. Even if the church community only had white members, it was not a result of discrimination against people of colour. Due to the Group Areas Act, it was impossible for people of colour to attend the services.

The Dutch Reformed Church (DRC) is an excellent example of how changing values and hierarchies as a result of the transition affect the reputation, opportunities, choices and positions of power and agency of specific institutions. The DRC continues to be an important social structure of the Afrikaner community in a context where Afrikaners have abandoned their claim on South Africa as their God-given land, have willingly surrendered power and are now a minority in their country of birth (Sparks 2003:17). One of the reverends argues that the question of guilt is very complex. Today, the DRC is in a difficult position because of its approval of apartheid, racial discrimination and exploitation based on the Bible. Nevertheless, the DRC also had clerics resisting apartheid, the four most prominent anti-apartheid spokespersons were: Beyers Naudé, Gert Swart, Ben

Marais and Willi Jonker. Today, there are of course feelings of guilt, but there are also feelings that the Truth and Reconciliation Commission (TRC) failed in certain instances and did not apply justice effectively in complicated situations. According to one DRC cleric, the TRC not only failed to address all the complexities and multifaceted aspects of apartheid but also refrained from investigating the atrocities committed by freedom fighters and the ANC, for example the different bombs and human rights violations in the camps. In the eyes of many Afrikaners, the TRC created a picture of them as perpetrators in a very simplistic and reductionist way, and this was not fair. On the other hand, there was also the problem of dealing with the TRC hearings. In particular, seeing certain members of the Afrikaner community exposed in front of the TRC was a challenging experience. These members had been role models, people they were proud of and people the Afrikaner community thought they could trust. To see that these people committed horrendous atrocities was difficult to accept. Nevertheless, current policies today are alienating Afrikaners from the government, even people who are willing to admit guilt. For example, affirmative action and the ideological underpinning of appointments are very alienating because they are seen as a new injustice. The worst part of these policies is that they provide Afrikaners who were very racist with a new reason to be racist. Hence, the development since 1994 is ambiguous and there are still people that are proud to be Afrikaners and those that are ashamed (interview 2007, 2008).

Other clerics argue that the transition has created opportunities but that reconciliation is a big challenge. It is possible to change the system quickly, but not the people, as they need more time to adapt. There is still widespread poverty, and a huge problem are the "nouveau riches" and their access to money and wealth. The accumulation of wealth becomes a priority and this has changed values of solidarity, honesty, commitment and empathy. At the grass-root level, there is still a daily struggle and there is an enormous need for help with basic issues such as food and shelter. In this environment of consumption and material values, community life is increasingly less important. Some people are bitter about the abuses of a well-intended transition, and there is little confidence in the government. Instead, there is the arrogance of the ruling party in manipulating things to suit them, for example the impunity of corrupt officials and government members. This context increases feelings of powerlessness and injustice. There is a great deal of despair among members of all racial groups (interviews 2006, 2007).

There is also a moral question around the Truth and Reconciliation Commission (TRC): murderers got away with the crimes they committed, whereas for poor people not much has changed, and they had to forgive the perpetrators. Politically, the TRC was a good compromise, but many issues have not been addressed, for example the beneficiaries of the old system, systemic discrimination and exploitation. Compensation payments are another problem that is unresolved. Some people have lost out in the transition and do not have the same privileges any more, but for many people, nothing has changed; there are many negative voices from both sides of the former divide. A number of clerics pointed out the fact that South African society is a social time-bomb. They argue that the lack of reconciliation affects inter-racial relations but also relations between the different socio-economic classes. This situation might one day spiral out of control. The government is not aware of the amount of anger in the population. In contrast, other clerics argue that poverty and deprivation in post-apartheid South Africa are more linked to ineffective policies and economic limitations as a result of globalisation. Hence, poverty and deprivation are increasingly less perceived as structural legacies of the past, which impacts on the willingness to rectify historical inequalities (interviews 2006, 2007).

Secularisation and Value Changes During the Transition and Democratisation

The various institutions of faith react to value changes. Nevertheless, the degree to which institutions of faith consider value changes as an opportunity or a threat varies. Engagement ranges from statements by clerics to their community to discussions and courses offered to community members during challenging times. Moreover, conservative communities tend to be united in the face of moral challenges, whereas in more liberal communities, tensions arise within the community, particularly between different generations. Challenges emanating from value changes influence levels of bonding. Contentious and contested issues concern the legalisation of abortion, same-sex marriages and euthanasia. Reactions are in some cases very emotional. Some clerics would never have thought that abortions or gay marriages would be legalised. The resultant changes of values and moral principles are a big concern, for example the legalisation of abortions potentially stimulating irresponsible behaviour. Hence religious institutions have a critical role in influencing and preserving values in the community, and providing guidelines. One cleric argues that religious rules do not change or adapt to social changes. Another cleric argues that the strict enforcement of religious rules would chase some people away and considers it more important that people are still part of the community (interview 2006, 2007).

Some churches are open to new values, for example same-sex marriages, but they are contested by conservative congregation members. In some churches openly gay couples are involved in church activities and are generally well accepted. Even in churches where people vehemently condemn same-sex marriages, openly gay couples involved in the community are valued as members of the community. In particular, elderly people are battling with the transformation and have the impression that there is neither choice nor space to influence changes. They feel powerless, and some people become bitter. In mainly middle class congregations, members are liberal and tolerant, also towards issues such as abortion or same-sex marriages. They differentiate between their own personal values and moral standards and those of other people, and they do not expect other people to adhere to the same principles. Some churches tolerate homosexuality; however, they do not sanction same-sex marriages. This might become a problem if gay couples ask for the blessings of the church (interviews 2006, 2007).

Courses and social activities offered to community members are important strategies to engage with transformation and changing values and to provide support structures and moral guidance. Activities differ and the various institutions present a range of options including, among others, discussions of Bible texts or books and discussions of topical issues such as education or marriage. A number of churches have discussion groups where issues such as abortion and same-sex marriages are addressed and related to the Bible (interviews 2006, 2007). In addition, all institutions of faith organise social events such as family days, tea for the elderly, youth groups or picnics.

All institutions of faith offer programmes for younger people to provide education and life skills regarding AIDS, sexuality and drugs. These programmes aim to protect young people, provide them with the necessary skills to react properly in challenging situations and strengthen their self-confidence and self-esteem so they are able to assert their rights and make informed decisions. More liberal churches are aware that it is impossible to prevent pre-marital sex. They consider it more important to accept these realities and support young people with advice instead of promoting abstinence and condemning young people who are sexually active. In contrast, other denominations offer "deliberately innocent" fun activities, and the Bible and the gospel are an important component of these activities to provide guidance and life-skills. The family as a principal institution of socialisation is highly valued. A number of clerics consider the disintegration of families in particular among the African population due to migrant work and the Group Areas Act the cause of many social ills such as crime, drug abuse or violence. Nevertheless, in the two neighbourhoods a considerable number of domestic workers live away from their families and only one cleric criticised the working and living conditions of domestic staff and their detrimental impact on family structures (interviews 2006, 2007).

For clerics from the Jewish community, the merits of the South African transition include the end of apartheid and discrimination, more opportunities and the democratisation of the state: in this respect, it was a big success. As one rabbi argued, the racism and discrimination of Blacks was appalling, and it was urgent that people got used to interacting with each other across former social divisions. People have more self-confidence today. In general, people are very patient and good persons. However, when it comes down to the daily practice, attitudes and prejudices have not changed as much yet. On the negative side, inequality has not been reduced. Now other groups are privileged, so this is a form of reverse racism. Definitively, morals have changed for the worse; during the old regime, there was no discussion of abortion or same-sex marriages. Moreover, everyone is affected by the same problems, for example crime, dishonesty, fraud and corruption. The prospects for change are slim because the government denies many problems, not only the magnitude of the AIDS crisis or the problems in Zimbabwe but also the effects of crime. The government is arrogant, complacent and lacks accountability because the ANC has a majority (interviews 2007).

For the Muslim community as a previously disadvantaged population group, the situation has positively changed. There are challenges, but Islam has answers to the problems and difficulties of the transition and provides values and norms that inform social relations. Islam is a very peaceful religion full of respect for life. Hence, it is important to clarify the misperception, misunderstanding and generalisation regarding Islam and religious practice. Islam is not militancy, violence and the Jihad. The hostilities towards the Muslim community all over the world and the reputation of Muslims as violent fighters, in particular after the September 11 attacks, are a problem (interview 2006).

Relations to Society and the State

Charity is the most prominent way religious institutions connect and interact with the wider society. Despite the engagement of various religious groups in the struggle, today the Norwood and Orange Grove institutions of faith are not involved in politics. However, there is a significant number of Jewish people individually involved in community organisations; both ward councillors and the chairpersons of the Norwood Community Police Forum and of the Norwood Orchards Residents' Association are Jewish.

Crime affects religious and social life in the community, and all institutions of faith are affected by crime. All interview partners state that crime destroys human interactions, affects levels of trust, makes people suspicious and affects relations with other racial groups or strangers. Walls become higher and higher, people refrain from walking in the neighbourhood and they often do not know their neighbours. There were incidents of crime during church services, for example handbags being stolen when church members went to the front to receive communion. It was easy to assume that the thieves were strangers or newcomers, so it is difficult under these circumstances to welcome new members. All communities have been affected by crime: cars were broken into or stolen during services, and many of their members have had personal experiences with crime, with cases ranging from burglaries to assault and rape. There was a general consensus among the interview partners that government responses to poverty and crime are inadequate and constitute one of the major failures of the new government. Today, the communities are not as close as they used to be, levels of solidarity have decreased and there are less structures of social control. Levels of crime are related to inequality, poverty, unemployment, lack of education and levels of illiteracy. The empowerment of the poor is critical, in particular of children and women. There are too many people that have no future, and that have no positive perspective of what to do with their lives.

Most institutions of faith work together with the Community Police Forum. For example, the police offer advice to congregation members on crime prevention. Programmes for domestic workers on issues of safety and security are very popular. The churches join forces with the CPF to increase security around the church venues. Nevertheless, representatives of the churches do not attend the monthly CPF meetings; they interact with the police and the CPF on a bilateral basis.

People relate personal well-being to state capacity. The dominant party and current power structures together with lacking accountability and transparency contribute to growing feelings of powerlessness and a less optimistic view of the future. Economic uncertainty and insecurity increase levels of stress and anxiety and affect the quality of social relations. Conservative religious institutions insulate themselves from the social environment. They are attractive for people struggling to adjust to rapidly changing values and norms, and they provide them with an environment that is less challenging and more predictable.

Jewish and Muslim communities have a strong sense of belonging, which is enforced by religious practices that differ from mainstream society: for example, food taboos, Friday prayers and the Sabbath. In addition, in both communities there are considerable measures of social control. Often, the social life of Muslims and Jews evolves primarily within the religious community. Charity mainly benefits members belonging to the respective religious community, which is easier to accomplish than in Christian communities because membership is more visible and communities are much smaller. The Muslim and Jewish communities provide safety nets for their members in personal or financial difficulties and help to alleviate hardship as a result of the transition. Moreover, both communities also provide educational or health facilities. Since members of both communities are strongly involved in the business sector and both communities also provide education and health facilities, there are also job opportunities. Membership in the two religious communities has many advantages, which in turn strengthen the sense of belonging.

In Conclusion – Institutions of Faith and Transformation

Institutions of faith are important community structures that promote social values, solidarity and compassion and offer spaces in the two neighbourhoods, where the different population groups can meet. Institutions of faith engage with the changing social and political environment as a result of the transition and provide important support structures to their members, in particular to individuals struggling to adapt to the transformation. However, the various institutions of faith differ in terms of their engagement with society or disconnection. All institutions of faith in the two neighbourhoods are confronted with the fundamental problems of post-apartheid South Africa: race relations, alienation between different population groups and reconciliation, inequality, poverty and crime. These problems are a challenge to democratic consolidation. They also affect daily social interactions, not only at the societal level but also between members of the different religious communities. Institutions of faith offer support structures and provide a sense of stability.

There is a strong division between religion and state; however, individual members of a number of institutions of faith are very active in their secular community and local politics. In addition, institutions of faith promote values and set normative standards, but they are not actively involved in putting them into practice. In general, the clerics are hesitant to speak out and mobilise the community in response to problems or social conflicts; they prefer to adopt a wait and see position. The levels of engagement with the different challenges vary considerably and reactions to moral conflicts such as the legalisation of same-sex marriages are out of proportion when compared to the reluctance to speak out on problems such as poverty and inequality. Conversely, all institutions of faith included in this study accept the new political and social order. Despite disagreement and possible disengagement, they adapt to the transformation and do not try to obstruct or undermine it. Institutions of faith offer support structures, but it is questionable whether they contribute to appeasement or strengthen social stability. Moreover, social relations are not as tense and conflictual in religious communities because the stakes are not as high as they are in neighbourhoods.

7 Five Years Later – What Has Changed?

Assessing Transformation

Transformation refers to the adaptation of individuals and social groups to changes that are the result of the political transition. As a consequence, the adjustment of social hierarchies and the rearrangement of access to power, opportunities and resources affect social relations between the various population groups. Transformation is necessary to enable previously privileged and disadvantaged population groups to respect one another and cooperate in a context of different priorities and concerns. Indicators of change are levels of integration, the heterogeneity of social organisations and networks in terms of racial, gender, class and age group representativeness. In addition, change is reflected in different expectations and challenges that affect priorities, strategies and perceptions of well-being, safety and order. Contestation arises between commitments to change and transformation and the perpetuation of the status quo, especially in a context where privileged groups have little incentive to transform a system that benefits them. Moreover, heterogeneity provides for the representation of different interests, but it still does not eliminate the unequal access to power of local actors and their weight in local organisations and political processes.

Strangely enough in 2006, at the beginning of the fieldwork, Norwood and Orange Grove were in two different local government wards. The two neighbourhoods not only have a shared history, they also developed around two important community institutions: the Paterson Park Recreation Centre and Grant Avenue, located along the boundaries between the two neighbourhoods. Moreover, the Paterson Park Recreation Centre and Grant Avenue are two major urban development projects that ironically focus on integration. In contrast to the ward delimitation, the Norwood Police station serves both neighbourhoods. The reassessment of ward boundaries prior to the 2011 municipal elections resulted in a readjustment, and both neighbourhoods are now integrated into Ward 73.

Demographics have also changed. In Ward 73, where Norwood and Orange Grove are located, population numbers are as follows:

Africans	Coloureds	Indians	Whites
12616	636	5006	10449

(based on Census 2011, Statistics South Africa)

The number of non-white residents has significantly increased, and according to the 2011 census only about 35 per cent of residents are white. It is not possible to compare these numbers directly to the Ward 73 and Ward 74 statistics of the 2001 Census. Moreover, the statistics of 2001 and 2011 include a larger area than the two neighbourhoods, and the distribution of the different racial groups varies within the area. However, these numbers also indicate a clear trend towards more diversity and the question arises how far the different community institutions and social networks reflect this trend in terms of representativeness and community development priorities.

The heterogeneity of social groups and institutions, in particular of social structures that are involved in local political processes, is an indicator of transformation. Heterogeneity not only reveals levels of racial integration but also includes gender, socio-economic class and age groups because these various population groups also have different needs and aspirations. Consequently, heterogeneity is an important indicator of inclusive representation in local processes, and as a normative characteristic it reflects the commitment to transformation. In local communities, development objectives and programmes also disclose the vision of an idealised community, the openness towards transformation and the importance assigned to inclusiveness and socio-economic integration. Perceptions of causes of problems in the neighbourhood and subsequent strategies to address them are further indicators of attitudes towards transformation, in addition to the language used to discuss community affairs or refer to specific population groups.

There is significant leverage in the decentralised structures of the local community to control access to local civil society and political institutions. Also, in official community networks, social relations do not only occur in formal settings, on the contrary, there is considerable space for manipulation in informal structures and informal channels to facilitate the uneven dissemination of information, gate-keeping, patterns of exclusion and victimisation or the promotion of dominant, universalised values. In informal settings, social interactions are less transparent and beyond measures of social control or obligations of accountability. The boundaries between the personal and formal are blurred and shifting as it is legitimate to have personal friendships and relations in the neighbourhood; however, these relations can be used to promote a specific agenda or manipulate local processes. Limited state capacity, the devolution of power and the promotion of local communities as agents of development strengthen the power and influence of dominant local networks and individuals.

Politics and Democratisation

The legacies of apartheid, especially the massive levels of inequality, remain an enormous challenge for the government. Expectations of the population are still high; nevertheless, patience and understanding for the slow pace of change are strained. The situation is exacerbated by poor service delivery, corruption and the conspicuous consumption of the political elite. Popular discontent fuelled by disappointment and frustration is manifest not only in the number of protests but also in the outbursts of violence and destruction during protest action. Political engagement and interactions between the government and the people occur very often outside democratic structures. The dominance of the ANC and the lacking commitment to engage with critique or investigate corruption limit trust in democratic institutions and the prospects of development, yet, people are at the same time still attached to the former liberation movement and continue to vote for the ANC. The largest opposition party, the DA, is gaining grounds, but not sufficiently to challenge the overwhelming majority of the ANC. The ambiguity of this situation is for example reflected in incidences at the local level, where people vote for the ANC and sometimes protest the very next day against the newly elected local government.

There are also more problematic developments caused by the lack of a consolidated democratic culture, different perceptions of and expectations from democracy but also by disrespect for democratic institutions, the undermining of democratic processes and the lack of transparency and accountability. The continuous attempts of interfering with or limiting a free and independent media are worrying. The critical role of the media in disclosing corruption and maladministration challenges and enrages the political elite, and instead of engaging with the issues or problems revealed by the press, offenders on the contrary choose to attack and discredit the media. In local elections conflicts between ANC candidates nominated by the party and ANC candidates nominated by the people are not resolved via the ballot box but instead by intimidation of the candidate and supporters, pressure on the people's candidate to withdraw or the expulsion from the party. There is lack of transparency in decision making processes, selective information dissemination, gate-keeping, the gerrymandering of local government delimitations and the lacking political will to engage with different opinions and critique. Manipulative practice occurs on all levels of political and civil society structures from the top down to local government wards and neighbourhoods.

Due to the legacies of apartheid and the extent of inequality, there are limitations to change. People have high expectations and there is also acknowledgement of progress, for example in the provision of housing, water and electricity or the social grant system. Nevertheless, the patience of the majority of poor people is strained, especially in the context of maladministration or the misappropriation of public funds and often incidences of corruption or conspicuous consumption overshadow successful government programmes. Moreover, such incidences violate the people's sense of justice and in a context of dire poverty and lacking opportunity, anger and frustration lead to outbursts of violence and destruction. Poverty alleviation, homelessness and unemployment are the biggest challenges, and all local communities are affected. As it is impossible to confront these problems effectively in local political institutions, local communities tend to remove the poor, homeless or informal traders at the expense of another community. Inequality produces latent conflicts and comprehensive national strategies are required to address the challenges of poverty, unemployment and homelessness. In all socio-economic groups assessments of government performance are based on the quality of services and inroads made in poverty alleviation, job creation or crime prevention. Despite widespread consensus about the challenges South Africa is facing, strategies to address these problems vary considerably between the various population groups. However, there was also opposition to government programmes uniting the population across all social and economic boundaries, for example the introduction of toll roads in Gauteng province.

Nearly twenty years into democracy, the pace of development is slow, the party landscape has not significantly changed and also within parties transformation is limited. Many of the same literally old faces dominate decision making structures in political institutions and parties. According to the 2011 census, nearly 50 per cent of the South African population is under 25 years old, nearly 73 per cent is under 40 years old; the age group over 40 years old that dominates politics constitutes only 27 per cent of the population (based on Census 2011, Statistics South Africa). It is not only the limited generational renewal within the parties, but also the programmes and even the slogans that have not changed which convey the impression of a certain stagnation. The DA is the most diverse party as regards racial representation. The dominance of the ANC together with the lacking renewal within party structures produce a certain indifference towards politics and confidence in the power of the vote. For the first time after twenty years into democracy, an entire generation of citizens born after the demise of apartheid will participate in the 2014 national elections.

The Neighbourhood – Continuities and Change

The most significant change in the two neighbourhoods is the influx of non-white residents, which has changed the racial composition, and, within the non-white group, the number of Indian residents has significantly increased. Other changes, for example the

Figs. 19 and 20: Houghton Residential Development

Houghton estate residential development or the improvement of Paterson Park with a planned housing scheme, are at least partly driven by the private sector. In both cases, community consultations are dominated by a small group of active residents claiming to represent the community. In the case of the Houghton estate, this small group was not affected by the negative consequences of the project such as noise and disruption during the construction phase or a massive increase in traffic with the number of apartments available on the estate. There is still resentment among affected residents about the ex-clusive way community consultation processes were conducted, moreover, they now face a luxury estate across the road while the public infrastructure on their side is decaying.

Governmental development plans move at a slower pace. One of the major struggles in both neighbourhoods is the maintenance and improvement of the existing infrastructure. The conversion of Grant Avenue into an activity street has not yet materialised. There were improvements to Spar and the shopping area around Spar and Woolworths is thriving, which has a positive impact of businesses along Grant Avenue. The number of coffee shops has increased and the Ascot Hotel has been upgraded and converted into a four star establishment. On the downside, it was not possible to mobilise and win the approval of a critical mass (51 per cent) of property and business owners along Grant Avenue to set up a City Improvement District. Continuous challenges are the number of informal traders especially around Spar and Woolworths; however, the fixed installation with shelves for merchandise at the corner of Grant Avenue and Ivy Road is now in good use.

There were also changes along Louis Botha Avenue. A number of new small businesses have opened, for example a bakery and a small take away shop. Supersconto, the Italian supermarket, has undergone some renovations and expanded. The shop has moved from the 3rd floor to street level and established a small coffee shop on the 1st floor. The bead store has moved across the road to smaller premises and the number of traditional healers has decreased. Due to the pressure exerted by the Orange Grove Residents' Organisation, illegal liquor outlets had to close. In contrast to Grant Avenue, Louis Botha is a main transit corridor. The projected Bus Rapid Transit line in Louis Botha Avenue from the city centre to Alexandra is welcomed by the local residents and according to the Orange Grove Residents' Association's chairperson it is as yet unclear whether buildings and land will be expropriated. A public meeting was planned to discuss the matter further, and there are also many derelict buildings along Louis Botha that could be demolished (Cox, iol, 2011). Business opportunities increase along Bus Rapid Transit lines as well as property values and the competition for urban space.

The planned changes to the Paterson Park Recreation Centre, especially the opening of the premises towards Grant Avenue, have not yet materialised; however, there were

Fig. 21: Public Infrastructure Across the Road of the Houghton

repairs and improvements to the buildings of the centre. The dilapidated public swimming pool has disappeared by filling it up and major improvements to the playground in Paterson Park have been implemented. But the same lady from the police barracks still looks after the outside area of the barracks. Increasing problems have emerged with the subletting of rooms or flats in the police barracks, significantly increasing the number of residents in the two buildings; overcrowding of houses is also a problem in Orange Grove West. The projected development of Paterson Park with the Art Complex and an urban agricultural training centre will contribute to the uplifting of the northern Orange Grove West residential area. Safety and security continue to be major challenges; there is still an extensive reliance on private security companies and road closures with controlled access to public spaces persist. Nevertheless, none of the planned major security clusters were implemented.

Community Organisations and the Representation of Residents

According to one of the residents, people in both neighbourhoods used to know each other, and it was not necessary to organise events in order for residents to meet their neighbours. This has changed a great deal (interview 2013). The lack of information structures makes it difficult to disseminate information, and not all residents have access to email or read the various community newspapers. In addition, social interactions across social boundaries develop slowly, and people are still alienated from one another. South Africa's history influences social relations, and experiences of the past not only affect assessments of the present but also make it difficult to adapt to dominant values and perceptions of order and security that were shaped by history. It is difficult for victims of apartheid to be part of and feel responsible towards a society that has failed them. This in turn contributes to the development of a one-sided relationship with the community where one can selectively take what is available without any consideration of also contributing to that society (Shahi, A. 2010).

People are reluctant to get involved in the community, besides which limited communication channels, disinterest and little faith in the impact of local organisations prevent community engagement. Consequently, the lacking interest in community affairs facilitates the formation of exclusive groups claiming to represent the community and dominating development processes. Such community organisations base their legitimacy on the absence and disengagement of other residents, arguing that everyone has the opportunity to get involved. Certain privileges, for example having more access to information, determining priorities or taking decisions, are derived from the effort, time and work invested in the community that nobody else is prepared to commit to. There is a thin line between the promotion of the collective good and the promotion of a specific agenda as the collective good. Moreover, in voluntary organisations requirements of transparency and accountability are at the discretion of individuals or the group, enabling the manipulation of processes or the exclusion of unwanted people. Strategies range from side-lining, gate-keeping, the selective dissemination of information, secrecy, discrediting or ridiculing people with a different opinion to attacks in the media or in social networks.

The diversity of the neighbourhood and the demographic changes since the abolishment of the Group Areas Act are not reflected in community organisations. It is difficult to cut across social boundaries, and continuities of the past affect social networks and their racial composition. The ward committees are still not well established and active organisations; people tend to get involved in organisations to which they are traditionally more attached, for example the residents' or business associations or the ward structures of the political parties. As these organisations existed already during South Africa's divided past, they are racially not yet integrated; likewise, gender and generational representation as well as the inclusion of different socio-economic groups are limited.

The Community Police Forum (CPF) has survived despite difficulties and challenges. A small dedicated group is very active, quite visible, cooperating with the police and trying to motivate more residents to get involved. A few non-white members have joined. In order to improve security and reduce crime, the promotion of sector policing is also a strategy to relate better to the residents of the different local areas and the security concerns they have. Problems of order and law enforcement, especially with respect to the poor, homeless and informal traders, influence perceptions of safety and stability.

Fig. 22: Stalls on Ivy Road

The impossibility to effectively address the persistent problem of poverty, unemployment and homelessness at the local level results in a cycle of driving the poor away from the neighbourhood until they return again. One of the non-white members of the CPF raised the question of what value residents add to the community and asked community members who complained about their own investments in the community. During the discussion it was argued that people can't just voice demands or profit from society without getting involved and make their contribution. As already stated, South Africa's divided past makes it difficult for people to feel responsible towards a society that has failed them.

The residents' associations of Orange Grove and Norwood, together with the Johannesburg Property Agency, have formed a Joint Oversight Committee which acts as a public forum and is open for input from the communities. In a way it is a concentration of power around the same small group already very active during the first phase of the field-work. Information about the activities of the Joint Oversight Committee are available on the internet. Nevertheless, access to the group is more difficult and limited; the CPF as well as the Councillor complained about the withholding or selective dissemination of information. A City Improvement District is planned along Louis Botha Avenue, which will become more competitive with the projected Bus Rapid Transit. The Joint Oversight Committee is also the driving force behind the Paterson Park development in cooperation with the City of Johannesburg. Not only the boundaries between government and the private sector lack transparency, there is also a conflict of interest: the chairperson of the Joint Oversight Committee is also involved in the project with his private business (www.bluerhino-design.com 2014). Apparently, the City of Johannesburg has provided one million Rand funding for the Paterson Park development. However, the Councillor has no information about the utilisation of the money. Decentralisation and the lacking capacity of the state facilitate the creation of a structure parallel to the elected political unit, the ward, and allows a small group of people to dominate the agenda of community development.

The ward committee and the councillor are the only elected structure in the community and are accountable to the entire community. Challenges are the different expectations of people in terms of development objectives and the limited resources and support from the state. The slow pace of development is frustrating. As a DA Councillor, it is a challenge to do justice to all residents of the ward, irrespective of their party preferences or affiliation. Prejudices that DA Councillors do not care for non-DA members or expectations that DA affiliates have more weight are difficult to balance. The DA has no party structure in the ward.

The influx of non-white residents is reflected in the emergence of an ANC Youth League (ANCYL) branch and an ANC ward structure in Ward 73, the John Nkadimeng Branch. Activities of the ANCYL vary and levels of engagement are related to the mobility levels of members. They engage with the councillor, demands are often linked to economic grievances and the quest for a more radical redistribution. The Paterson Park Recreation Centre was also involved in a dispute, as the ANCYL was incensed that they had to pay in order to use a room and they demanded free access for the community to the centre.

The John Nkadimeng Branch is active and one of the focal areas is the problem of urban poverty. A member of the branch argued that there are neither reliable figures available to assess the extent of urban poverty, nor is there a specific debate about poverty in the city that could contribute to the development of more comprehensive and sustainable poverty alleviation strategies. Housing in the area, especially affordable housing is another focus of the branch's activities. There is already a shortage of housing and many flats and houses are overcrowded. The planned Bus Rapid Transit will increase the value and attractiveness of the properties along Louis Botha, which are currently the home of thousands of less affluent residents. As the majority of the properties along Louis Botha are in dire need of investment and renovation, there are concerns that the properties will be sold to developers and subsequently people will get evicted.

The quality of communication with other community structures varies but it is impossible to get information from the Joint Oversight Committee and it is even less feasible to join the committee despite the fact that the Joint Oversight Committee claims to be open for input from the communities and to act as a public forum. As is the case with civil society structures, there is in the official and observable management of the City of Johannesburg also space for informal, less detectable social dynamics. Limited transparency and personal relations between dominant residents and city structures facilitate the support of a highly visible but blatantly exclusive community structure at the expense of a more inclusive approach to community development. Unfortunately, conflicts of interest between holders of public or community offices and their businesses are not only fairly frequent, often there is little or no objection by the community or political institutions against such practices.

Schools

The situation of the public schools in the area has not improved. Despite high commitment and investment in education by the government, the impact is limited. In 2010,

19.20 % of government spending was allocated to education, that is 5.98% of GNI (indexmundi.com). Beside the expenditure, access and the quality of education are further indicators of the state of education in South Africa. Furthermore, the allocation of resources within the different educational sectors are additional relevant aspects.

According to the World Economic Forum's 2013 Report on Global Information Technology, South Africa is ranked as follows:

Quality of Education 140 of 144 (ahead of Haiti, Libya, Burundi, Yemen)
Maths and Science 143 of 144 (ahead of Yemen)
Secondary Enrolment 56 of 144
Adult Literacy 93 of 144
(Bilbao-Osoria et al. 2013:324-327)

Moreover, three government departments are involved in education: basic education, higher education and training, and science and technology. The administration around education is well intended but also takes a good part of the resources allocated to the sector at the expense of competitive teachers' salaries and the size of classes. It impacts on trust in and the reputation of the public education system, the motivation and commitment of teachers and the levels of burn-outs and absenteeism. For most parents, the education of their children is highly valued, which is reflected in the efforts they take to offer their children quality education, for example enrolling them in public schools of wealthier suburbs. This is understandable, as education is also widely seen as one of the routes out of poverty; however, it does not resolve the educational crisis in the country, on the contrary, the problems are delegated to the individual schools, which struggle to maintain their standards of education. The situation in the four schools in this study has become more precarious. Government compensations in order to make up for parents unable to pay school fees continue to be below actual fees and impact on and drain school resources. Moreover, the government can force schools to admit more learners and thus increase the size of classes, making it challenging to maintain standards of education.

Religious Institutions

The influx of Indians into the neighbourhoods also changed the presence of the different religious denominations. The 2011 census did not collect data on the religious affiliation of South Africans, nevertheless, the growing Muslim community is visible, first and foremost by the completed new building of the mosque, the Masjid Ul Furquan, in 2nd Street across the road of the Houghton Estate. The presence of a growing Muslim community also has an impact on businesses and consumer goods.

The Jewish community is still present in the neighbourhood, but there is a trend of moving towards Sandringham, Sydenham and Glenhazel, and according to one of the interview partners, more than 90 per cent of residents in Glenhazel are Jewish. There are no major changes among the Christian denominations except for a modest decline in Pentecostal churches along Louis Botha Avenue.

Local Communities: Participation, Representation and Transformation?

Transformation is a challenging and slow process. South Africa's history affects community development and limits transformation as different social structures try to promote, manipulate or prevent changes. The continuous alienation between the different population groups and persistent levels of inequality hinder the emergence of more integrated community structures. Community structures do not reflect the diversity of the two neighbourhoods. In this context, decentralisation paved the way for well connected, articulate and dominant community members and groups to promote and pursue a specific agenda that serves particular interests. The lack of state capacity, the reliance on community networks and the promotion of public private partnerships contribute to a situation where decentralisation undermines the democratisation process and prevents the formation of a more inclusive community with shared development objectives that benefit all.

Fig. 23: Masjid Ul Furquan

8 Conclusion – Transformation from Below?

Political transitions are characterised by uncertainty and instability. They are negotiated in a context of opportunities and limitations, and they potentially result in a regime change and not in a structural transformation of the state. South Africa is an example of a relatively successful transition. The democratisation of the state has resulted in changes that affect access to power, the distribution of resources, opportunities and burdens, the rearrangement of social hierarchies, the transformation of values and norms and the reputation of the various population groups. Nonetheless, South Africans differ in terms of their responses and willingness to adjust to the consequences of the transition. Hence, transformation is not an automatic or logical result of political transition. Transformation is a conscious and committed effort to adapt, integrate and accept the consequences of the transition with its effects on one's life, the social environment and relations with other individuals and groups. This is a challenge in a context where the various population groups have different priorities and aspirations and where structural and systemic inequalities due to the legacies of apartheid perpetuate discrimination, influencing the space of agency.

This study of a formerly white residential area in Johannesburg demonstrates the contested and conflictual practical aspects of transformation. In contrast to the political sphere, there is space for continuities of the past in the social realm; social capital in formal and informal relations between individuals and groups is a critical element in this context. Local networks and organisations not only differ in terms of their priorities and aspirations, inequalities are also reflected in the weight and bargaining leverage of individuals and social groups and the various resources they are able to access. Social relations facilitate cooperation but also enable the pursuit of specific interests and a particular agenda at the expense of the public good. Hence, the state has to protect collective development objectives by constraining powerful social groups and by promoting the interests of less resourceful and influential groups. In an environment of conflicting interests and high levels of inequality, where privileged population groups are reluctant to change arrangements that benefit them, only the state has the autonomy and power to promote collective development objectives.

Local development and social interactions occur in a broader societal context. Social relations are influenced by economic conditions, political stability and government capacity as well as perceptions of safety, security and a sense of control. Insecurity and instability increase both risks and stakes for individuals and groups, intensify the competition for resources and raise levels of conflict. Nevertheless, development is only possible without social exclusion and without the marginalisation of less powerful population groups. Development depends on the state's capacity to secure basic rights and decent living conditions for the entire population, and its ability to address inequality, poverty and related social problems such as crime and violence. The three focus areas of this study, namely the local communities and their local political institutions, the schools and the institutions of faith, illustrate the different potentials for tensions, contention and conflict that correlate with perceived threats, unpredictability and precariousness.

In neighbourhoods, the stakes in the environment are high, and the range of alternatives is limited and costly. Moving elsewhere is not easy, and other areas may potentially have similar challenges because there are constraints on individual levels of control, influence and space of agency. The cooperation with other people is imperative because neighbourhood development and the addressing of problems exceed individual agency. Nevertheless, the reliance on specific networks and financial resources allows structures to develop that limit cooperation with the state and population groups with different development priorities. Social and financial capital enables the promotion of an agenda that undermines the public good and serves the interests of a minority. In addition, the avoidance of the state is attractive to population groups that have less access to political power as a result of the transition.

The 2011 census clearly shows that demographics have changed and more non-white residents live in the area. However, Norwood and Orchards Residents' Association, the Orange Grove Residents' Association as well as the Grant Avenue and Louis Botha Avenue Business Associations do not reflect the heterogeneity of the community and are not representative. On the contrary, they consciously exclude certain population groups, for example tenants and informal businesses. Their development objectives are limited and guided by particular interests at the expense of integrated development. Not only civic organisations but also the ward committees are dominated by a specific agenda and do not represent the community's diversity. The mobilisation for ward committee elections is a problem due to the absence of information channels and the lacking interest of community members to get involved. The mobilisation of community members occurs mainly through personal relations, which allows for more informal and less transparent processes. Councillors, the political parties or dominant community members are in a powerful position to approach people they would like to join the ward committee. Consequently, specific interest groups not only dominate the community and determine development priorities, they also set normative standards regarding order, decency and appropriate behaviour.

Apartheid's legacies and its patterns of stringent control influence perceptions of order and the utilisation of public space. These standards discriminate against the poor and homeless because they do not fit into conceptions of a desirable community; development strategies are not concerned with problems of inequality and poverty. Since poor and homeless people are mainly black, patterns of exclusion also have a strong racial dimension. The City Improvement District along Louis Botha Avenue and the Orange Grove West/Victoria/Fellside Urban Management District or the Joint Oversight Committee are valid examples of projects that not only serve specific development objectives in the interest of a particular group, they also simultaneously facilitate the removal of unwelcome population groups from the neighbourhood. The promotion of public-private partnerships increases the problem because the private sector is more concerned with economic and not social aspects of development.

Decentralisation and the promotion of participatory structures in local communities are a problem in an environment of pervasive inequalities. The reliance on local networks as agents of development is dangerous in a context of conflicting interests and unequal access to power and resources. Furthermore, problems such as widespread poverty or unemployment are impossible to resolve in local political structures. Decentralisation critically depends on the capacity of the central state to avoid the fragmentation of local communities and the shift of power to dominant local actors. The problem of fragmentation is exacerbated by the state's attitude that more affluent communities should look after themselves and in its promotion of the private sector in development projects.

Even the mobilisation around the common interest of crime prevention does not result in a significantly more integrated community structure. The Community Police Forum (CPF) is dominated by the white middle class, and genuine efforts to integrate other population groups were not very successful; five years later there is only a small number of non-white community members involved. Moreover, race is a factor because most community members involved in the CPF are white and the police are mostly black. The racial division between the two structures becomes more problematic through the racialised perception of crime. The CPF also illustrates the ambiguous relationship with state institutions. There is little trust in the capacity of the state not only when it comes to effectively reduce levels of crime but also to resolve other problems contributing to disorder and instability. Negative assessments of state capacity are enforced by perceptions of corruption. Lacking state capacity vindicates the resort to services outside the state, for example the questionable promotion of private security. It also limits incentives for cooperation between the state and communities.

Stakes are also high in schools because education is valued by all population groups. Parents are concerned about the education of their children; nevertheless, this common interest does not translate into integrated social structures or vibrant social networks around schools and the demand for quality education. The three public schools investigated in this study exemplify the enormous changes in terms of resources, composition of learners and problems that affect schools, factors that all contribute to the worsening reputation of public schools. Paterson Park Primary, the independent Seventh Day Adventist School, is in a similar situation. Education is important, but alternatives to public schools are easily accessible and promise more favourable education outcomes for population groups with the necessary purchasing power. Hence, the transfer to private schools is a viable option. The trend towards private schooling limits conflict levels and pressures on the public education system because influential and powerful population groups do not depend on it. Conversely, less affluent and disadvantaged population groups lack the necessary resources to afford better educational opportunities for their children. The crisis in public schools perpetuates inequalities by reducing prospects for less privileged learners.

The four schools in this study are not integrated and do not reflect the heterogeneity of the two neighbourhoods, neither in terms of racial composition nor in terms of socio-economic class. Furthermore, the preference for private schools also has an impact on neighbourhood sociability. In contrast to public schools, parental engagement is high in private schools but has no effect on neighbourly relations because these social structures do not overlap with locality. In addition, education increases agency and choices, raises levels of self-esteem and self-confidence and influences the nature of social relations. Education also increases the propensity for civic engagement as is aptly demonstrated by the correlation of education levels, civic engagement, dominance and influence of specific individuals and community groups in the two neighbourhoods of this study.

Institutions of faith offer spaces where the different population groups can meet. In addition, institutions of faith provide guidance and support structures to individuals and groups struggling to adapt to the rapidly changing environment as a result of the South African transition. Religious principles and values are common denominators for people from different racial and socio-economic groups and personal backgrounds. As a result, religion unites people, and social capital is high in religious institutions. Levels of conflict are low and stakes not as high as in schools or neighbourhoods: people tend to leave rather than confront their religious community in cases of conflict. Spirituality and membership in institutions of faith are valued in South Africa, and their support structures contribute to social stability. Religious institutions provide mutual support structures but they are not involved in the neighbourhood. Despite the engagement with questions of inequality, reconciliation and value changes within their communities, institutions of faith do not contribute to structural changes or comprehensive transformation. Clerics of religious institutions included in this study neither speak out nor confront the state. They do not, for instance, debate the collective challenges of social transformation or address burning issues such as inequality, poverty or corruption. On the contrary, religious institutions are the main providers of charity as a moral obligation towards the less fortunate. It is argued that charity neglects controversial issues such as citizenship rights and social inclusion and does not confront the roots of inequality. As the most prominent civil society structures, religious institutions contribute to the vibrancy of associational life but their impact on politics is limited in post-apartheid South Africa.

In general, the different interview partners acknowledged the objective limitations to change and transformation, but they criticised government priorities, the allocation of resources and the government's lacking transparency and accountability. Social relations and interactions are affected by levels of stability, predictability and the quality of politics. Economic instability and insecurity are major concerns, and economic grievances and threats increase tensions, raise levels of conflict and affect personal well-being. Different interview partners articulated the problems that emanate from an unpredictable and precarious personal economic context and the threat to livelihoods and pointed at the experiences of unskilled workers or community members with limited educational qualifications. In addition, party loyalty, personal networks and nepotism were considered unfair in relation to job opportunities and the allocation of government tenders. These machinations are facilitated by a lack of transparency and accountability and they violate people's sense of justice. The situation is exacerbated by the lifestyle and conspicuous consumption of politicians and the new business elite.

The consolidation of democracy in South Africa is also affected by low levels of trust in government and political institutions. People judge the quality of politics and government performance on the merits of service delivery and the behaviour and moral standards of the political elite. It is a problem when political leaders do not live up to people's expectations. Specifically, the limited commitment to accountability and transparency is criticised. The current imbalance of power and dominance of the African National Congress (ANC) contribute to negative perceptions of the state. Moreover, due to its dominance the ANC can ignore critique or manipulate democratic processes for example by pressuring communities to refrain from electing a candidate competing with the official selection of the party or by gerrymandering ward boundaries. The lack of an influential and viable opposition limits intervention options and increases feelings of powerlessness.

The capacity and impartiality of state institutions are critical conditions for political stability. They influence levels of social integration and quality of cooperation in the impersonal and complex environment of the modern state. Political trust does not operate at the individual level of social networks. Rather, it operates at the societal level and is reflected in the degree of confidence in state institutions and the government. A volatile social, political and economic environment, insecurity due to high levels of crime, biased law enforcement and corruption all influence the nature of social networks in communities. State capacity and consistency in maintaining safety and security, in enforcing the law and in creating political and economic stability influence civic behaviour and the respect of social norms by individuals. Civic attitudes depend on the voluntary compliance and cooperation of citizens, so it is impossible to enforce them.

Corruption affects relations within society and between citizens and the state. Moreover, violations of social norms by official malfeasance dominate perceptions of government performance, limiting the willingness of citizens to acknowledge and appreciate successful government programmes. All interview partners had experiences with corruption, and many pointed at the detrimental consequences of lacking accountability. The situation is worsened by limited electoral competition, incidents of arrogant leadership and perceptions that political office also serves personal interests and not only the community. Powerful people can afford to violate social norms. Moreover, institutional systems of checks and balances are considered inefficient and contribute to feelings of impunity by corrupt officials. Perceptions of limited state capacity, doubts concerning the integrity of politicians and the administration and low levels of political trust encourage and legitimise the necessity to rely on personal social relations and networks, to promote a specific agenda or develop parallel structures that undermine elected institutions.

Personal networks become increasingly important when the state fails to address challenges and vital problems. In this context of lacking capacity and disorder, more privileged individuals with access to powerful and dominant social organisations and networks have more bargaining leverage and space of agency. They can influence local political processes or avoid cooperation with the state. The weaker state institutions are, the more successful local networks and organisations become. However, these organisations and networks are not embedded in society and exclude specific population groups. This situation is exacerbated by intolerable levels of crime and therefore legitimate safety and security concerns. Nevertheless, the result is exclusive arrangements that privilege powerful individuals or groups. The Joint Oversight Committee including the Norwood and Orange Grove Residents' Association and the Johannesburg Property Agency provide a good example of a small group that represents the community and influences priorities and development goals. It is not only difficult to distinguish between collective and individual aspirations, boundaries between the government and the private sector are blurred and there are conflicts of interests between individuals active in the community and involved with their businesses. Ultimately, the Joint Oversight Committee created a parallel structure to the elected ward committee and the councillor.

Cooperation between citizens and between citizens and the state is less conflictual and easier in more egalitarian societies. Moreover, there is little faith in the impact of local community engagement, hence people are reluctant to get involved. This facilitates not only the formation of exclusive networks, these structures also claim to represent the community. Their legitimacy is based on the absence of other community members as everyone would have the opportunity to get involved. Inclusive cooperation therefore depends on government strategies that address the problem of inequality. Social networks can become a destructive resource in a context of pervasive inequalities because poor people lack the voice and bargaining leverage to advance their interests. They depend disproportionately on state support to promote their demands and address their grievances. Furthermore, effective strategies to alleviate poverty and inequality are a fundamental condition of transformation and democratic consolidation in South Africa. A certain level of socio-economic conditions is not only required for people to exercise their democratic rights, it is also guaranteed by the constitution. For the majority of South Africans discriminated and oppressed by apartheid, expectations of democracy inseparately equate political rights with socio-economic rights and are fundamentally linked to redistribution and redress. In the two neighbourhoods of this study, the middle class has an ambiguous relationship with the poor and homeless. Current approaches to poverty alleviation separate the poor from the rest of society. Shifting the focus away from the poor to the problem of inequality and the question of redistribution allows for the inclusion of the entire population in the transformation process. This approach emphasises the interdependence of the various population groups because successful and sustainable poverty alleviation programmes need the support of the entire population.

Different interview partners argued that governmental strategies of poverty alleviation are not successful because the number of poor people has not significantly decreased. Limitations on job creation and the promotion of individual entrepreneurship and creativity in an increasingly volatile global economic context together with the moral value attached to work contribute to impressions that poverty and unemployment are also the result of irresponsible behaviour and thereby obscure the incapacity of the South African government to effectively address the problem of unemployment. The moralisation of work also distracts from the most burning social problems that emanate from the fundamentals of the post-industrial labour market: namely that full, permanent employment is a relic of the past and that structural unemployment will increase.

Levels of diversity arising from cultural differences and economic inequalities that characterise post-apartheid South Africa are a challenge to community development: the various population groups have different needs and aspirations. Transformation and cooperation depend less on social networks in decentralised structures than on the acknowledgement that the different groups are interdependent and that sustainable development is not feasible without each other. This study illustrates the marginalisation of less powerful social groups and the poor in local communities where access to resources is unevenly distributed. Local political processes confirm the central role of the state, not only in addressing the underlying systemic and structural conditions that limit development but also in promoting an inclusive development vision that is the responsibility of the entire population in order to promote transformation as a collective objective that benefits all.

Appendix

Fieldwork in Norwood and Orange Grove

The fieldwork is based on interviews and participant observation. It presents a diversity of social networks with different purposes, interests, viewpoints and levels of engagement in the community and with the local administration. However, only a limited number of social structures, networks and organisations overlap with the specific geographical locality. Local social structures are necessary for interest aggregation, mobilisation and cooperation in the neighbourhood; hence a stake in the community was the decisive selection criterion. The focus is only on formal social structures and includes community and public institutions, schools and institutions of faith:

> the Norwood Community Police Forum,
> the Norwood and Orchards Residents' Association (NORA),
> the Orange Grove Residents' Association
> the business associations of Grant Avenue and Louis Botha Avenue.

Norwood and Orange Grove are in two different local government wards, the most de-centralised political structures. Both ward councillors have been interviewed as well as members of the ward committees and members of the two most active political parties in the area, the African National Congress (ANC) and the Democratic Alliance (DA).

Orange Grove historically had a large Italian immigrant community, and both neighbourhoods have a considerable number of Greek immigrants; hence both immigrants' organisations have been included in the study.

Community institutions were incorporated, namely the two libraries and the Paterson Park Recreation Centre in Norwood which is actively involved in community development programmes. The local old age home is included in addition to Lifeline, a crisis support structure, and CARE, the Community AIDS Response. Both Lifeline and CARE are located in the neighbourhood but serve a much larger area.

Schools have been included for various reasons. Schools are embedded in the neighbourhood and hence contribute to the social life in local communities. School activities bring people together and provide information channels regarding community events and support structures. In addition, education contributes to empowerment and enhances future opportunities of formerly discriminated populations. In schools, the common experiences of children from different racial backgrounds contribute to social integration.

The four schools included in this study are: Norwood, Orange Grove, Houghton and Paterson Park Primary School.

Institutions of faith are included because 43 per cent of the population are members of a religious institution. This is the highest membership proportion in comparison to any other civil society organisations (wa Kivilu 2002:125). Institutions of faith are based in the community, provide spaces where people from different social groups and economic backgrounds can meet and encourage social relations and social engagement. On the other hand, the secularisation of the state and the promotion of liberal values reflected in democratic values, civil liberties and gender equality potentially conflict with values cherished by institutions of faith, for example perceptions of gender roles within the hierarchical, patriarchal structures of religious institutions.

Interviews were conducted with clerics and members of different Christian denominations and members of the Jewish and Muslim communities.

The focus of the interviews was on the activities, programmes and priorities of the different community structures and the challenges, problems and difficulties they face. The quality of communication and cooperation with political institutions and the City of Johannesburg administration were assessed. This assessment included the responsiveness and accountability of the political and administrative authorities. All interviews with representatives of community institutions, schools and institutions of faith were qualitative, in-depth, semi-structured and based on open questions, allowing participants to include whatever they considered important. No questionnaires were used; however, there was a set of questions providing a guideline. Interviews were conversations rather than "question-answer" sessions.

The interview partners were mainly in a leading position and not ordinary members of the respective civil society structures. With a few exceptions, most community members I approached were forthcoming and willing to talk to me about the community and their engagement in it. The different racial groups are unevenly represented in this study: the over-representation of white interview partners reflects the levels of transformation and the representation of non-white community members is weak. The anonymity of interview partners was as far as possible protected. In the case of elected officials and prominent and active community members it may be possible for readers to identify them. There is no confidential material or issues included that interviewees considered private. However, I also think that community members, whether in elected institutions or community based organisations, which are involved and participate in the development of the neighbourhood, claim to represent the community, interact and take part in planning and decision making processes with the local government and administration or receive funding from the local government have a responsibility to inform and interact with the local population. Hence, for residents in elected positions or in leadership functions in community institutions a certain exposure is not only unavoidable but also a requirement of transparency and accountability.

Interviews have been conducted between May 2006 and October 2008. A second set of interviews has been conducted between July 2013 and January 2014 at least five years later of the original fieldwork to follow-up on the developments in Norwood and Orange Grove. Generally, the people I have approached in connection with the interviews were very cooperative and very open in answering my questions, even when we touched on sensitive issues. The noteworthy exception was an extremely prominent and active community member who avoided talking to me from the beginning of my fieldwork. Nevertheless, it was not too difficult to collect more information, a number of interview partner smentioned him in their interviews with me, either because they are pleased with his engagement in the community or they are upset about his domineering leadership style, the selective dissemination of information and the side-lining or exclusion of people who contest or confront him. Moreover, his internet presence provided further information.

Acronyms and abbreviations

ALEX	Alexandra Township
ANC	African National Congress
ANCYL	African National Congress Youth League
BEE	Black Economic Empowerment
CID	City Improvement District
COSATU	Congress of South African Trade Unions
CPF	Community Police Forum
DA	Democratic Alliance
DRC	Dutch Reformed Church
GEAR	Growth Employment and Redistribution
HIP	Hellenic, Italian and Portuguese umbrella organisation
LBBA	Louis Botha Business Association
NCPF	Norwood Community Police Forum
NGO	Non-Governmental Organisation
NORA	Norwood and Orchards Residents' Association
RDP	Reconstruction and Development Programme
PTA	Parent-Teacher Association
SACP	South African Communist Party
TRC	Truth and Reconciliation Commission
UMD	Urban Management District

Bibliography

Adam, H., Slabbert, F., Moodley, K. 1997. *Comrades in Business*. Cape Town: Tafelberg Publishers.

Adler, G., Steinberg, J. 2000. Introduction: From Comrades to Citizens, in Adler, G., Steinberg, J. (Editors) 2000. *From Comrades to Citizens*. London: Macmillan.

African National Congress. 1994. *Reconstruction and Development Programme*. Johannesburg: Umanyano Publications.

Altbeker, A. 2005. *The Dirty Work of Democracy*. Johannesburg and Cape Town: Jonathan Ball Publishers.

Amin, A., Graham, S. 1999. Cities of Connection and Disconnection, in Allen, J., Massey, D., Pryke, M. 1999. *Unsettling Cities*. London and New York: Routledge.

Anonymous, 1983. No title, *North Eastern Tribune*, 20 September 1983

Anonymous, 1986. Well-Pointed Norwood Has Very Small Lot Sizes But Fetches High Prices, *The Star*, 29 September 1986.

Anonymous, 1988. Open Areas No Problem in Norwood, *Five Freedoms Forum*, October 1988.

Anonymous, 2006. Fear Factor, *Economist*, 3 August 2006.

Back, L., Keith, M. 2004. Impurity and the Emancipatory City: Young People, Community Safety and Racial Danger, in Lees, L. (Editor) 2004. *The Emancipatory City?*. London: Sage Publications.

Ballard, R. 2004. Middle Class Neighbourhoods or "African Kraals"? The Impact of Informal Settlements and Vagrants on Post-Apartheid White Identity, *Urban Forum*, Vol. 15, No. 1, 2004.

Bayart, J.F. 1999. The 'Social Capital' of the Felonious State, in Bayart, J.F., Ellis, S., Hibou, B. (Editors) 1999. *The Criminalisation of the State in Africa*. Oxford: James Currey.

Beall, J., Crankshaw, O., Parnell, S. 2002. *Uniting a Divided City*. London: Earthscan.

Beavon, K. 2004. *Johannesburg The Making and the Shaping of the City*. Pretoria: University of South Africa Press, Leiden: Koninklijke Brill NV.

Beinart, W. 1994. *Twentieth-Century South Africa*. Oxford: Oxford University Press.

Bell, T., Ntsebeza, D.B. 2001. *Unfinished Business South Africa Apartheid and Truth*. Observatory, Muizenberg: RedWorks.

Berman, S. 1997. Civil Society and the Collapse of the Weimar Republic, *World Politics*, Vol. 49, No. 3, 1997.

Bilbao-Osorio, B., Dutta, S., Lanvin, B. (Editors) 2013. *The Global Information Ychnology Report 2013*. Published by WEF and INSEAD (retrieved from internet 2 February).

Blowers, A., Pain, K. 1999. The Unsustainable City?, in Pile, S., Brook, C., Mooney, G. 1999. *Unruly Cities?*. London and New York: Routledge.

Boggs, C. 2002. Social Capital as Political Fantasy, in McLean, S.L., Schultz, D.A., Steger, M.B. (Editors) 2002. *Social Capital Critical Perspectives on Community and "Bowling Alone"*. New York: New York University Press.

Boix, C., Posner, D. N. 1998. Social Capital: Explaining Its Origins and Effects on Government Performance, *British Journal of Political Science*, Vol. 28, No. 4, 1998.

Bourdieu, P. 1983. The Forms of Capital, in Richardson, J.G. (Editor) 1996. *Handbook of Theory and Research for the Sociology of Education*. New York: Green Press.

Bourdieu, P. 1988. *Outline of a Theory of Practice*. Cambridge: Cambridge University Press.

Bourdieu, P. 1998. *Practical Reason On the Theory of Action*. Cambridge: Polity Press.

Bourdieu, P. (Edited and Introduced by Thompson, J.B.) 2005. *Language and Symbolic Power*. Cambridge: Polity Press.

Bourdieu, P., Passeron, J.C. 1996. *Reproduction in Education, Society and Culture*. London: Sage Publications.

Bourdieu, P., Wacquant, L.J.D. 1996. *An Invitation to Reflexive Sociology*. Cambridge: Polity Press.

Bratton, M., Mattes, R. 2004. What "The People" Say About Reforms, in Gyimah-Boadi, E. (Editor) 2004. *Democratic Reform in Africa*. Boulder, London: Lynne Rienner Publishers.

Briggs, X. 1997. Social Capital and the City: Advice to Change Agents, *National Civic Review*, Vol. 86, No. 2, 1997.

Bruce, H.J. 1983. Talk to the Mountain View Resident Association AGM held on 14 September 1981, *Journal of the Johannesburg Historical Foundation*, Vol. 4, No. 1, September 1983.

Chhibber, A. 2000. Social Capital, the State and Development Outcome, in Dasgupta P., Serageldin, I. (Editors) 2000. *Social Capital: A Multifaceted Perspective*. Washington DC: World Bank.

Chidester, D., Dexter, P., James, W. (Editors) 2003. *What Holds Us Together Social Cohesion in South Africa*. Cape Town: HSRC Press.

Cleaver, F. 2001. Institutions, Agency and the Limitations of Participatory Approaches to Development, in Cooke, B., Kothari, U. (Editors) 2001. *Participation The New Tyranny?* London, New York: Zed Books.

Cloete, F. 1991. Greying and Free Settlement, Swilling, M., Humphries, R., Shubane, K. (Editors) 1991. *Apartheid City in Transition.* Cape Town: Oxford University Press.

Coleman, J.S. 1988. Social Capital and the Creation of Human Capital, in *American Journal of Sociology* (Supplement), Vol. 94, No. S1, 1988.

Coleman, J.S. 1990. *Foundations of Social Theory.* Cambridge MA: The Belknap Press of Harvard University Press.

Coleman, J.S. 1992. The Rational Reconstruction of Society: 1992 Presidential Address, in *American Sociological Review.* Vol. 58, Issue 1, February 1993.

Colletta N.J., Cullen, M. L. 2000a. The Nexus Between Violent Conflict, Social Capital, and Social Cohesion: Case Studies from Cambodia and Rwanda, *World Bank*, Social Capital Initiative Working Paper No. 23.

Colletta N.J., Cullen, M. L. 2000b. *Violent Conflict and the Transformation of Social Capital.* Washington DC: World Bank.

Cooke, B., Kothari, U. 2001. The Case for Participation as Tyranny, in Cooke, B., Kothari, U. (Editors) 2001. *Participation The New Tyranny?* London, New York: Zed Books.

Costa, D.L., Kahn, M.E. 2001. Understanding the Decline in Social Capital, 1952-1998, *NBER Working Paper Series*, Working Paper 8295, May 2001.

Cox, A. 2011. *IOL.* http://www.iol.co.za/motoring/industry-news/goodbye-oxford-rd-hello-louis-botha-1.1168965#.UvxkY4W7InI (retrieved 26 January 2014).

Davenport, R. 1991. Historical Background of the Apartheid City to 1948, in Swilling, M., Humphries, R., Shubane, K. (Editors) 1991. *Apartheid City in Transition.* Cape Town: Oxford University Press.

Dekker, P. 2004. Social Capital of Individuals: Relational Asset or Personal Quality?, in Prakash, S., Selle, P. (Editors) 2004. *Investigating Social Capital Comparative Perspectives on Civil Society, Participation and Governance.* New Delhi, Thousand Oaks, London: Sage Publications.

Diani M. 2001. Social Capital as Social Movement Outcome, in Edwards, B., Foley, M., Diani, M. 2001. (Editors) *Beyond Tocqueville: Civil Society and the Social Capital Debate in Comparative Perspective.* Hanover, NH: University Press of New England.

Distiller, N., Steyn, M. (Editors) 2004. *Under Construction "Race" and Identity in South Africa Today.* Johannesburg: Heinemann.

Dupas, G. 2001. The Logic of Globalisation: Tensions and Governability in Contemporary Society, *Management of Social Transformation – MOST*, Discussion Paper 52, UNESCO, Social and Human Sciences.

Du Toit, F. 2003. *Learning to Live Together*. Cape Town: Institute for Justice and Reconciliation.

Edwards, B., Foley, M.W. 1997. Social Capital and the Political Economy of Discontent, *American Behavioural Scientist*, Vol. 40, Issue 5, March / April 1997.

Edwards, B., Foley, M.W. 1998. Civil Society and Social Capital Beyond Putnam, *American Behavioural Scientist*, Vol. 42, Issue 1, September 1998.

Edwards, B., Foley, M., Diani, M. 2001. (Editors) *Beyond Tocqueville: Civil Society and the Social Capital Debate in Comparative Perspective*. Hanover, NH: University Press of New England.

Egan, A. 2007. Kingdom Deferred? The Churches in South Africa, 1994-2006, in Buhlungu, S., Daniel, J., Southall, R., Lutchman, J. (Editors) 2007. *State of the Nation South Africa 2007*. Pretoria: Human Sciences Research Council Press.

Erasmus, Z. 2005. Race and Identity in the Nation, in Southall, R., Lutchman, J. (Editors) 2005. *State of the Nation South Africa 2004-2005*. Cape Town: Human Sciences Research Council.

Evans, P.B. 1996. Government Action, Social Capital and Development: Reviewing the Evidence on Synergy, *World Development*, Vol. 24, No. 6, 1996.

Evans, P.B., Rueschemeyer, D., Skocpol, T. (Editors) 1995. *Bringing the State Back In*. Cambridge: Cambridge University Press.

Fine, B. 1999. The Developmental State is Dead – Long Live Social Capital, *Development and Change*, Vol. 30, No. 1, January 1999.

Fine, B. 2001. *Social Theory Political Economy and Social Science at the Turn of the Millennium*. London and New York: Routledge

Fine, B., Green, F. 2000. Economics, Social Capital and the Colonisation of the Social Sciences, in Baron S., Field J., Schuller T. (Editors) 2000. *Social Capital: Critical Perspectives*. Oxford: Oxford University Press.

Foley, M.W., Edwards, B. 1997. Escape from Politics? Social Theory and the Social Capital Debate, *American Behavioural Scientist*, Vol. 40, Issue 5, March / April 1997.

Foley, M.W., Edwards, B. 1998. Beyond Tocqueville: Civil Society and Social Capital in Comparative Perspective, *American Behavioural Scientist*, Vol. 42, Issue 1, September 1998.

Foley, M.W., Edwards, B. 1999. Is It Time to Disinvest in Social Capital?, *Journal of Public Policy*, Vol. 19, No. 2, 1999.

Foley, M.W., Edwards, B., Diani, M. 2001. Social Capital Reconsidered, in Foley, M.W., Edwards, B., Diani, M. (Editors) 2001. *Beyond Tocqueville: Civil Society and Social Capital in Comparative Perspective*. Hanover: University Press of New England.

Foster, D. 2005. Racialisation and the Micro-Ecology of Contact, *South African Journal of Psychology*, Vol. 35, No. 3 2005.

Fraser, N. 1997. *Justice Interruptus*. New York and London: Routledge.

Fried, A. 2002. The Strange Disappearance of Alexis de Tocqueville in Putnam's Analysis of Social Capital, in McLean, S.L., Schultz, D.A., Steger, M.B. (Editors) 2002. *Social Capital Critical Perspectives on Community and "Bowling Alone"*. New York: New York University Press.

Friedman, S. 2004. South Africa: Building Democracy After Apartheid, in Gyimah-Boadi, E. (Editor) 2004. *Democratic Reform in Africa*. Boulder, London: Lynne Rienner Publishers.

Gibson, J.L., Gouws, A. 2003. *Overcoming Intolerance in South Africa*. Cambridge: Cambridge University Press.

Godfrey, D. 1974. Romantic History of Northern Suburb, *The Star*, 14 September 1974.

Gouws, A. 2002. The Importance of Political Tolerance for Fostering Social Cohesion, in Chidester, D., Dexter, P., James, W. (Editors) 2003. *What Holds Us Together Social Cohesion in South Africa*. Cape Town: HSRC Press.

Habib, A. 2003. Conversation with a Nation: Race and Redress in South Africa, in Pieterse, E., Meintjies, F. (Editors) 2004. *Voices of Transition The Politics, Poetics and Practises of Social Change in South Africa*. Johannesburg: Heinemann.

Habib, A., Schultz-Herzenberg, C. 2005. Accountability and Democracy, in Calland, R., Graham, P. (Editors) 2005. *Democracy in the Time of Mbeki*. Cape Town: IDASA.

Hadenius, A. 2004. Social Capital and Democracy, in Prakash, S., Selle, P. (Editors) 2004. *Investigating Social Capital Comparative Perspectives on Civil Society, Participation and Governance*. New Delhi, Thousand Oaks, London: Sage Publications.

Hall, P.A. 2002. Great Britain The Role of Government and the Distribution of Social Capital, in Putnam, R.D. (Editor) 2002. *Democracies in Flux*. Oxford: Oxford University Press.

Hall, S. 2002. Daubing the Drudges of Fury: Men, Violence and the Piety of 'Hegemonic Masculinity" Thesis, *Theoretical Criminology*, Vol. 6, No. 1, 2002.

Hamilton, K., Hoyle, S. 1999. Moving Cities: Transport and Connections, in Allen, J., Massey, D., Pryke, M. (Editors) 1999. *Unsettling Cities*. London and New York: Routledge.

Harrison, P. 2003. Fragmentation and Globalisation as the New Meta-Narrative, in Harrison, P., Huchzermeyer, M., Mayekiso, M. (Editors), 2003. Confronting Fragmentation Housing and Urban Development in a Democratising Society, Cape Town: UCT Press.

Harriss, J. 2002. *Depoliticising Development The World Bank and Social Capital*. London: Anthem Press.

Harriss, J., De Renzio, P. 1997. 'Missing Link' or Analytically Missing?: The Concept of Social Capital, *Journal of International Development*, Vol. 9, No. 7, 1997.

Hassim, S. 2006. *Women's Organisations and Democracy in South Africa Contesting Authority*. Scottsville: University of KwaZulu-Natal Press.

Hassim, S. 2006. Gender Equality and Developmental Social Welfare in South Africa, in Razavi, S., Hassim, S. (Editors) 2006. *Gender and Social Policy in a Global Context*. Basingstoke: Palgrave Macmillan.

Heller, P. 2001. Moving the State: The Politics of Democratic Decentralisation in Kerala, South Africa and Porto Alegre, *Politics and Society*, Vol. 29, No. 1, 2001.

Heller, P. 2003. Reclaiming Democratic Spaces: Civics and Politics in Posttransition South Africa, in Tomlinson, R., Beauregard, R.A., Bremner, L., Mangcu, X. (Editors) 2003. *Emerging Johannesburg*. New York, London: Routledge.

Heying, C.H. 1997. Civic Elites and Corporate Delocalisation: An Alternative Explanation for Declining Civic Engagement, *American Behavioural Scientist*, Vol. 40, Issue 5, March / April 1997.

Hildyard, N., Hedge, P., Wolvekamp, P., Reddy, S. 2001. Pluralism, Participation and Power: Joint Forest Management in India, in Cooke, B., Kothari, U. (Editors) 2001. *Participation The New Tyranny*? London, New York: Zed Books.

Hooghe, M., Stolle, D. (Editors) 2003. *Generating Social Capital*. New York: Palgrave.

Huysseune, M. 2003. Institutions and Their Impact on Social Capital and Civic Culture, in Hooghe, M., Stolle, D. (Editors) 2003. *Generating Social Capital*. New York: Palgrave.

Indexmundi

http://www.indexmundi.com/facts/south-africa/education-expenditure, (retrieved 25 January 2014).

Jacobs, J. 1961. *The Death and Life of Great American Cities*. London: Jonathan Cape.

Juergens, U., Gnad, M., Baehr, J. 2003. New Forms of Class and Racial Segregation: Ghettos or Ethnic Enclaves?, in Tomlinson, R., Beauregard, R.A., Bremner, L., Mangcu, X. (Editors) 2003. *Emerging Johannesburg*. New York, London: Routledge.

Khosa, M.M. 2002. Infrastructure and Service Delivery in South Africa, 1994-1999, in Parnell, S., Pieterse, E., Swilling, M., Wooldridge, D. (Editors) 2002. *Democratising Local Government the South African Experiment*. Cape Town: University of Cape Town Press.

Khosa, M.M. 2005. Participation and Democracy, in Calland, R., Graham, P. (Editors) 2005. *Democracy in the Time of Mbeki*. Cape Town: IDASA.

Kim, J.Y. 2005. "Bowling Together" Isn't a Cure-All: the Relationship between Social Capital and Political Trust in South Korea, *International Political Science Review*, Vol. 26, No. 2, 2005.

Koelble, T.A. 2003a. Building a New Nation: Solidarity, Democracy and Nationhood in the Age of Circulatory Capitalism, in Chidester, D., Dexter, P., James, W. (Editors) 2003. *What Holds Us Together Social Cohesion in South Africa*. Cape Town: HSRC Press.

Koelble, T.A. 2003b. Ten Years After: Robert Putnam and Making Democracy Work in the Post-Colony or Why Mainstream Political Science Cannot Understand Either Democracy or Culture, *Politikon*, Vol. 30, No. 2, November 2003.

Krishna, A. 2002. *Active Social Capital*. New York: Columbia University Press.

Krishna, A., Shrader, E. 1999. *Social Capital Assessment Tool*. Conference on Social Capital and Poverty Reduction, The World Bank, Washington D.C., 22-24 June 1999.

Kymlicka, W. 1996. *Multicultural Citizenship*. Oxford: Clarendon Press.

Kymlicka, W., Norman, W. 2000. Citizenship in Culturally Diverse Societies: Issues, Contexts, Concepts, in Kymlicka, W., Norman, W. (Editors) 2000. *Citizenship in Diverse Societies*. Oxford: Oxford University Press.

Lauglo, J. 2000. Social Capital in Trumping Class and Cultural Capital? Engagement with School among Immigrant Youth, in Baron S., Field J., Schuller T. (Editors) 2000. *Social Capital: Critical Perspectives*. Oxford: Oxford University Press.

Lefebvre, H. 1976. Reflections on the Politics of Space, *Antipode*, Vol. 8, No. 2, May 1976.

Leftwich, A. 1995. Bringing Politics Back in: Towards a Model of the Developmental State, *Journal of Development Studies*, Vol. 31, No. 3, February 1995.

Levi, M. 1996. Social and Unsocial Capital: A Review Essay of Robert Putnam's Making Democracy Work, *Politics and Society*, Vol. 24, No. 1, March 1996.

Leyds, G.A. 1964. *A History of Johannesburg*. Cape Town: Nasionale Boekhandel.

Lin, N. 2001. *Social Capital A Theory of Social Structure and Action*. Cambridge: Cambridge University Press.

Lodge, T. 1998. Political Corruption in South Africa, *African Affairs*, Vol. 97, Issue 387, April 1998.

Lodge, T. 2002. *Politics in South Africa, from Mandela to Mbeki*. Cape Town: David Philip.

MacDonald, M. 2006. *Why Race Matters in South Africa*. Pietermaritzburg: University of Natal Press.

Mahlangu, D. 2004. Norwood Cops Are Tops, *Sunday Times*, 6 June 2004.

Maloney, W., Smith, G., Stoker, G. 2000. Social Capital and Urban Governance: Adding a More Contextualised Top-Down Perspective, *Political Studies*, Vol. 48.

Maloney, W., Smith, G., Stoker, G. 2001. Social Capital and the City, in Edwards, B., Foley, M., Diani, M. 2001. (Editors) *Beyond Tocqueville: Civil Society and the Social Capital Debate in Comparative Perspective*. Hanover, NH: University Press of New England.

Mangcu, X. 2008. *To the Brink The State of Democracy in South Africa*. Scottsville: University of KwaZulu-Natal Press.

Mansbridge, J. 2000. What Does a Representative Do? Descriptive Representation in Communicative Settings of Distrust, Uncrystallised Interests and Historically Denigrated Status, in Kymlicka, W., Norman, W. (Editors) 2000. *Citizenship in Diverse Societies*. Oxford: Oxford University Press.

Marais, H. 2001. *South Africa's Limits to Change The Political Economy of Transition*. London and New York: Zed Books Ltd.

Mattes, R. 2002. South Africa: Democracy Without the People, *Journal of Democracy*, Vol. 13, No. 1, 2002.

Mayekiso, M. 2003. South Africa's Enduring Urban Crisis: The Local State and the Urban Social Movement with Particular Reference to Johannesburg, in Harrison, P., Huchzermeyer, M., Mayekiso, M. (Editors), 2003. *Confronting Fragmentation Housing and Urban Development in a Democratising Society*, Cape Town: UCT Press.

McDowell, l. 1999. City Life and Differences: Negotiating Diversity, in Allen, J., Massey, D., Pryke, M. (Editors)1999. *Unsettling Cities*. London and New York: Routledge.

McLaughlin, E., Muncie, J. 1999. Walled Cities: Surveillance, Regulation and Segregation, in Pile, S., Brook, C., Mooney, G. (Editors) 1999. *Unruly Cities?* London and New York: Routledge in association with The Open University.

McLean, S.L., Schultz, D.A., Steger, M.B. 2002. Introduction, in McLean, S.L., Schultz, D.A., Steger, M.B. (Editors) 2002. *Social Capital Critical Perspectives on Community and "Bowling Alone"*. New York: New York University Press.

Meintjies, F. 2004. Imperatives of Visionary Leadership, in Pieterse, E., Meintjies, F. (Editors) 2004. *Voices of Transition The Politics, Poetics and Practises of Social Change in South Africa*. Johannesburg: Heinemann.

Mohan, G. 2001. Beyond Participation: Strategies for Deeper Empowerment, in Cooke, B., Kothari, U. (Editors) 2001. *Participation The New Tyranny?*. London, New York: Zed Books.

Molyneux, M. 2002. Gender and the Silences of Social Capital: Lessons from Latin America, Development and Change, Vol. 33, No. 2, 2002.

Mosse, D. 2001. 'People's Knowledge', Participation and Patronage: Operations and Representations in Rural Development, in Cooke, B., Kothari, U. (Editors) 2001. Participation The New Tyranny? London, New York: Zed Books.

Mungazi, D.A., Walker, L.K. 1997. *Educational Reform and the Transformation of Southern Africa*. London: Praeger.

Murray, M.J. 2008. *Taming the Disorderly City The Spatial Landscape of Johannesburg After Apartheid*. Ithaca and London: Cornell University Press.

Naidoo, S. 2004. Park Fury, *Sunday Times*, 8 February 2004.

Naidoo, s., Eliseev, A., Mofokeng, L. 2004. Party 'Chaos', *Sunday Times*, 29 August 2004.

Nell, V. 2001. Community Psychology and the Problem of Policing in Countries in Transition, in Seedat, M. (Editor in consultation with Duncan, N., Lazarus, S.) 2001. *Community Psychology Theory, Method and Practice South African and Other Perspectives*. Oxford: Oxford University Press.

Neuhouser, K. 1995. "Worse Than Men": Gendered Mobilisation in an Urban Brazilian Squatter Settlements, 1971-91, *Gender and Society*, Vol. 9, No. 1, 1995.

Newton, K., Norris, P. 1999. Confidence in Public Institutions, in Pharr, S., Putnam, R. D. (Editors), 2000. *Disaffected Democracies: What's Troubling Trilateral Democracies?*. Princeton: Princeton University Press.

Nordlund, P. 1996. Democracy and Social Capital in a Segmented South Africa, in Agora Project, 1996. *Democracy and Social Capital in Segmented Societies*. Working Papers from the Conference on Social Capital and Democracy, India, March 1996.

Norris, P., Inglehart, R. 2003. Gendering Social Capital: Bowling in Women's Leagues?, *Conference on Gender and Social Capital*, St. John's College, University of Manitoba, 203 May 2003.

Offe, C. 1999. How Can We Trust Our Fellow Citizens?, in Warren, M. (Editor), 1999. *Democracy and Trust*. Cambridge: Cambridge University Press.

Offe, C. 2000. Political Liberalism, Groups Rights and the Politics of Fear and Trust, Conference Paper, Ben Gurion University, Israel, May 19-21, 2000.

Paterson, L. 2000. Civil Society and Democratic Renewal, in Baron S., Field J., Schuller T. (Editors) 2000. *Social Capital: Critical Perspectives*. Oxford: Oxford University Press.

Pendock, N. 1999. Radium Leaves Patrons with a Happy Glow, *Sunday Times*, 11 April 1999.

Pieterse, E. 2002. Participatory Local Governance in the Making, in Parnell, S., Pieterse, E., Swilling, M., Wooldridge, D. (Editors) 2002. *Democratising Local Government the South African Experiment*. Cape Town: University of Cape Town Press.

Pieterse, E. 2003. Unravelling the Different Meanings of Integration: The Urban Development Framework of the South African Government, in Harrison, P., Huchzermeyer, M., Mayekiso, M. (Editors), 2003. *Confronting Fragmentation Housing and Urban Development in a Democratising Society*, Cape Town: UCT Press.

Pieterse, E. 2004. Sketches of Development Praxis Against a Horizon of Complexity, in Pieterse, E., Meintjies, F. (Editors) 2004. *Voices of Transition The Politics, Poetics and Practises of Social Change in South Africa*. Johannesburg: Heinemann.

Pieterse, E., Meintjies, F. 2004. Introduction: Framing the Politics, Poetics and Practices of Social Change in the New South Africa, in Pieterse, E., Meintjies, F. (Editors) 2004. *Voices of Transition The Politics, Poetics and Practises of Social Change in South Africa*. Johannesburg: Heinemann.

Portes, A. 1998. Social Capital: Its Origins and Applications in Modern Sociology, *Annual Review of Sociology*, Vol. 24, 1998.

Portes, A. 2000. The Two Meanings of Social Capital, *Sociological Forum*, Vol. 15, No. 1, 2000.

Portes A., Landolt, P. 1996. The Downside of Social Capital, *The American Prospect*, Vol. 26, May-June 1996.

Portes, A., Sensenbrenner, J. 1993. Embeddedness and Immigration: Notes on the Social Determinants of Economic Action, *American Journal of Sociology*, Vol. 98, No. 6, 1993.

Prakash, S., Selle, P. (Editors) 2004. *Investigating Social Capital Comparative Perspectives on Civil Society, Participation and Governance*. New Delhi, Thousand Oaks, London: Sage Publications.

Prakash, S., Selle, P. 2004. Introduction: Why Investigate Social Capital?, in Prakash, S., Selle, P. (Editors) 2004. *Investigating Social Capital Comparative Perspectives on Civil Society, Participation and Governance.* New Delhi, Thousand Oaks, London: Sage Publications.

Przeworski, A. 1995. *Sustainable Democracy.* Cambridge: Cambridge University Press.

Putnam, R.D., (with Leonardi, R. Nanetti, R.Y.) 1993. *Making Democracy Work Civic Traditions in Italy.* New Jersey: Princeton University Press.

Putnam, R.D. 1993. The Prosperous Community, *The American Prospect*, Vol. 4, Issue 13, March 21, 1993.

Putnam, R.D. 1995. Bowling Alone: America's Declining Social Capital, *Journal of Democracy*, Vol. 6, No. 1, 1995.

Putnam, R.D. 1996. The Strange Disappearance of Civic America, *The American Prospect*, Vol. 7, Issue 24, December 1, 1996.

Putnam, R.D. 2000. *Bowling Alone.* New York: Touchstone.

Putnam, R.D, 2002. Bowling Together, *The American Prospect*, Vol. 13, Issue 3, February 1, 2002.

Putnam, R.D. (Editor) 2002. *Democracies in Flux.* Oxford: Oxford University Press.

Putnam, R.D. 2007. E Pluribus Unum: Diversity in the Twenty-First Century, The 2006 Johan Skytte Prize Lecture, *Scandinavian Political Studies*, Vol. 30, No. 2, 2007.

Robinson, J. 1997. The Geopolitics of South African Cities, *Political Geography*, Vol. 16, No. 5, 1997.

Robinson, J. 1998. Spaces of Democracy: Remapping the Apartheid City, *Environment and Planning D: Society and Space*, Vol. 16, 1998.

Robinson, J. 1999. Divisive Cities: Power and Segregation in Cities, in Pile, S., Brook, C., Mooney, G. (Editors) 1999. *Unruly Cities?.* London and New York: Routledge.

Robinson, J. 2003. Johannesburg's Future: Beyond Developmentalism and Global Success, in Tomlinson, R., Beauregard, R.A., Bremner, L., Mangcu, X. (Editors) 2003. *Emerging Johannesburg.* New York, London: Routledge.

Robinson, J. 2006. *Ordinary Cities Between Modernity and Development.* New York: Routledge.

Rothstein, B. 2002. Sweden Social Capital in the Social Democratic State, in Putnam, R. D. (Editor) 2002. *Democracies in Flux.* Oxford: University Press.

Rothstein, B. 2004. Social Capital and Institutional Legitimacy: The Corleone Connection, in Prakash, S., Selle, P. (Editors) 2004. *Investigating Social Capital Compara-*

tive Perspectives on Civil Society, Participation and Governance. New Delhi, Thousand Oaks, London: Sage Publications.

Rothstein, B., Stolle, D. 2003. Social Capital, Impartiality and the Welfare State: An Institutional Approach, in Hooghe, M., Stolle, D. (Editors) 2003. *Generating Social Capital*. New York: Palgrave.

Rubio, M. 1997. Perverse Social Capital, *Journal of Economic Issues*, Vol. 31, No. 3, 1997.

Schaerf, W., Saban, G., Hauck, M. 2001. Local Communities and Crime Prevention: Two Experiments in Partnership Policing, in Steinberg, J. (Editor) 2001. *Crime Wave*. Johannesburg: University of the Witwatersrand Press.

Scheidegger, U. 2004. *Social Capital Its Beneficial and Destructive Potential in Post-Apartheid South Africa*. Unpublished Masters Thesis, Johannesburg: University of the Witwatersrand.

Seekings, J. 2000. *The UDF A History of the United Democratic Front in South Africa 1983-1991*. Oxford: James Currey.

Sennett, R. 1976. *The Fall of the Public Man*. Cambridge: Cambridge University Press.

Sennett, R. 2003. *Respect The Formation of Character in an Age of Inequality*. London: Penguin Books.

Shahi, A. 2010. The Failure of British Multiculturalism and the Virtue of Reciprocity, *e-International Relations*, 9 December 2010.

Shapiro, M.J. 1997. Bowling Blind: Post Liberal Civil Society and the Worlds of Neo-Tocquevillean Social Theory, in McLean, S.L., Schultz, D.A., Steger, M.B. (Editors) 2002. *Social Capital Critical Perspectives on Community and "Bowling Alone"*. New York: New York University Press.

Sharieff A. (Chief Editor), Khan, M.A., Balakishan, A. (Editors) 2007. *Encyclopaedia of World Geography Volume 17 Geography of South Africa*. New Delhi: Sarup and Sons.

Shaw, M. 2002. *Crime and Policing in Post-Apartheid South Africa Transforming Under Fire*. Cape Town: David Philip Publishers.

Siisiäinen, M. 2000. *Two Concepts of Social Capital: Bourdieu vs. Putnam*, Conference Paper presented at the ISTR Fourth International Conference, Trinity College, Dublin, Ireland, 5-8 July 2000.

Simone, A.M. 2002. The Dilemmas of Informality for African Urban Governance, in Parnell, S., Pieterse, E., Swilling, M., Wooldridge, D. (Editors), 2002. *Democratising Local Government The South African Experiment*, Cape Town: University Press.

Simone, A.M. 2004. People as Infrastructure: Intersecting Fragments in Johannesburg, *Public Culture*, Vol. 16, No. 3, Fall 2004)

Smith, A.H. 1971. *Johannesburg Street Names*. Johannesburg: Juta and Company Limited.

Sparks, A. 1994. *Tomorrow is Another Country*. Sandton: Struik Publishing Group.

Sparks, A. 2003. *Beyond the Miracle*. London: Profile Books Ltd.

Steger, M.B. 2002. Robert Putnam, Social Capital and a Suspect Named Globalisation, in McLean, S.L., Schultz, D.A., Steger, M.B. (Editors) 2002. *Social Capital Critical Perspectives on Community and "Bowling Alone"*. New York: New York University Press.

Steinberg, J. 2001. Introduction: Behind the Crime Wave, in Steinberg, J. (Editor) 2001. *Crime Wave*. Johannesburg: University of the Witwatersrand Press.

Steyn, M.E. 2001. *"Whiteness Just Isn't What It Used To Be" White Identity in a Changing South Africa*. Albany: State University of New York Press.

Stolle, D. 2003. The Sources of Social Capital, in Hooghe, M., Stolle, D. (Editors) 2003. *Generating Social Capital*. New York: Palgrave.

Stolle, D. 2004. Communities, Social Capital and Local Government, in Prakash, S., Selle, P. (Editors) 2004. *Investigating Social Capital Comparative Perspectives on Civil Society, Participation and Governance*. New Delhi, Thousand Oaks, London: Sage Publications.

Stolle, D., Soroka, S., Johnston, R. 2008. When Does Diversity Erode Trust? Neighbourhood Diversity, Interpersonal Trust and the Mediating Effect of Social Interactions, *Political Studies*, Vol. 36, Issue 1.

Suttner, R. 2006. *African National Congress (ANC) as Dominant Organisation: Impact of the Attainment of Power and Phases of Post Liberation Development and Crisis*, paper presented on 25 August 2006, University of the Witwatersrand.

Tarrow, S. 1996. Making Social Capital Work Across Space and Time: A Critical Reflection on Robert Putnam's Making Democracy Work, *American Political Science Review*, Vol. 90, No. 2, June 1996.

Taylor, V. 2002. *Transforming the Present – Protecting the Future Committee of Inquiry into a Comprehensive System of Social Security*. Pretoria: Government of South Africa.

Taylor, V. 2003. Epilogue: Contesting the Terrain in Paradoxical Landscapes?, in Pieterse, E., Meintjies, F. (Editors) 2004. *Voices of Transition The Politics, Poetics and Practises of Social Change in South Africa*. Johannesburg: Heinemann.

Terreblanche, S. 2002. *A History of Inequality in South Africa 1652-2002*. Pietermaritzburg: University of Natal Press.

Tihanyi, K. 2006. *Blending in the Rainbow*. Lanham, MD: Lexington Books.

Unsworth, A. 2000. Down in the Grove, *Sunday Times*, 12 March 2000.

Usher, H.J. 1973. The Story of Little Italy, *The Star*, 8 October 1973.

Uslaner, E.M. 1999. Democracy and Social Capital, in Warren, M.E. (Editor) 1999. *Democracy and Trust*. Cambridge: Cambridge University Press.

Uslaner, E.M. 2002. *The Moral Foundations of Trust*. Cambridge: Cambridge University Press.

Wa Kivilu, M. 2002. Civil Society Participation, in no author/editor, 2002. *Public Attitudes in Contemporary South Africa*, Cape Town: Human Sciences Research Council.

Warren, M.E. (Editor) 1999. *Democracy and Trust*. Cambridge: University Press.

Watson, A. 2007. Grand Grant Planned, *Eastern Tribune*, 11 May 2007.

Watson, S. 1999. City Politics, in Pile, S., Brook, C., Mooney, G. 1999. *Unruly Cities?*. London and New York: Routledge

Whiteley, P.F. 1999. The Origins of Social Capital, in Van Deth, J.W., Maraffi, M. Newton, K., Whiteley, P.F. (Editors) 1999. *Social Capital and European Democracy*. Routledge: London and New York.

Woolcock, M. 1998. Social Capital and Economic Development: Toward a Theoretical Synthesis and Policy Framework, *Theory and Society*, Vol. 27, No. 2, 1998.

Woolcock, M., Narayan, D. 2000. Social Capital: Implications for Development Theory, Research, and Policy, *The World Bank Research Observer*, Vol. 15, No. 2, 2000.

Worms, J.P., 2002. France Old and New Civic and Social Ties in France, in Putnam, R.D. (Editor) 2002. *Democracies in Flux*. Oxford: Oxford University Press.

Wuthnow, R. 2002. United States Bridging the Privileged and the Marginalised?, in Putnam, R.D. (Editor) 2002. Democracies in Flux. Oxford: Oxford University Press.

Young, I.M. 1990. *Justice and the Politics of Difference*. Princeton, New Jersey: Princeton University Press.

Government Sources

City of Johannesburg Council, 2004. Regional Spatial Development Framework, Sub Area Twenty Two, 16 September 2004.

Department of Finance, 1996. *Growth, Employment and Redistribution A Macroeconomic Strategy*.

Republic of South Africa, 1998, Government Gazette, Vol. 397, No. 18739, 13 March 1998. Notice 423 of 1998, White Paper on Local Government.

Statistics South Africa, 2006. Population Census 2001, Pretoria

Websites

www.bluerhino-design.com (retrieved 24 January 2014)

www.bluerhino-design.com/about-bluerhino.htm (retrieved 24 January 2014)

www.indexmundi.com/facts/south-africa/education-expenditure
(retrieved 25 January 2014)

www.mobilitate.co.za (retrieved 20 Janaury 2014)

www.iol.co.za/motoring/industry-news/goodbye-oxford-rd-hello-louis-
botha-1.1168965#.UvxkY4W7InI (retrieved 26 January 2014)

Speeches

Mandela, N.R. 1997. Mr Mandela: 50th National Conference of the ANC, *Report by the President of the ANC, Mr Mandela*, Speech held at the 50th National Conference of the ANC in Mafikeng on 16 December 1997.

Index

A

accountability XV, 1 f., 5 f., 13, 18–23, 44, 49, 51–53, 71, 73, 78, 108 f., 112 f., 118, 127 f.

adaptation VIII f., 82, 111

African Initiated Church 97

African National Congress (ANC) XV f., 7, 12–15, 20 f., 23, 52, 70–73, 78, 89, 105, 108, 113 f., 120, 127

African National Congress Youth League (ANCYL) 120

agency XV, 3 f., 7, 17 f., 22, 44, 54, 77, 81, 96, 104, 124, 126

Anglican Church 100

apartheid VIII, X f., XV, XVII, 1, 4, 11–21, 28 f., 31, 36, 38 f., 45, 47, 49, 53, 61, 70, 82, 91, 98–100, 103 f., 107, 113 f., 117, 123, 129

B

Bantu Education Act 80

Bantustan 14

Baptist Church 100 f.

basic rights 124

Beall, Jo 36, 50

Beavon, Keith 25–30

Bourdieu, Pierre XIII, 2 f., 12, 82, 97

Briggs, Xavier XIII

business XIV, XVI, 27–29, 33 f., 41 f., 49, 58, 64–67, 72, 74, 78, 83, 93, 109, 116, 118 f., 127

Bus Rapid Transit 116, 119 f.

C

Catholic Church 75 f., 100

change VIII–X, XVII, 1, 6, 11, 13, 20, 47, 61, 66, 105 f., 108, 111, 113 f., 123, 127

charity 76, 100, 102 f., 127

checks and balances 5 f., 22, 128

Christian XIV, XVI, 85, 91, 95, 97–100, 102–104, 109, 122

citizen XII–XIV, XVI, 6, 9, 11, 16, 21–23, 39, 43 f., 52 f., 61, 69 f., 74, 104, 114, 128 f.

city X, XII f., 19, 24–30, 32, 41, 46, 49, 66, 68–70, 77, 80, 103, 116, 120

City Council 33 f., 37, 46 f., 63, 66 f., 69, 71

City Improvement District (CID) 31 f., 63, 65–67, 116, 119, 125

civil liberties 16, 95, 99

civil rights 4, 23

civil society XI, XIV, XVI, 1–7, 9, 12, 15, 19 f., 23, 50, 55, 64, 95, 98, 102, 112 f., 120, 127

client 7, 51, 55

community XI–XVII, 1 f., 4, 6, 8 f., 17–20, 24, 28, 30, 35, 39, 43, 44–49, 51–53, 55–61,
     63–66, 69–78, 81 f., 92–102, 104–112, 114 f., 117–122, 124–130

Community Police Forum (CPF) XIV f., 41, 45 f., 49, 51–53, 55–60, 71, 78, 108 f.,
     118 f., 125

conflict X f., XIII–XVI, 3 f., 7, 9, 15, 17 f., 24, 40, 45 f., 48, 52, 61, 64–66, 68, 74, 81,
     87 f., 92, 96, 99, 102 f., 110, 113 f., 119 f., 124, 126 f., 129

Congress of South African Trade Unions (COSATU) 12, 14 f.

constitution 76, 129

control VIII–XI, XV, 1, 4, 8, 12, 21 f., 24, 26, 29, 39, 43 f., 48, 50, 53 f., 61 f., 71, 78 f., 91,
     96, 106, 112, 123–125

cooperation X–XII, XVI, 2, 4, 7, 14, 41, 44, 49, 52 f., 55 f., 58, 61, 67, 71, 80 f., 90 f., 119,
     123–125, 128–130

corruption 19, 21–23, 52 f., 61, 73, 78, 108, 113 f., 125, 127 f.

councillor 69, 71, 119 f., 129

crime XV, 7 f., 17 f., 33, 40, 43–45, 48 f., 52 f., 55 f., 61, 71, 73, 78, 99, 107–110, 114, 118,
     124 f., 128

D

decentralisation XI f., 1, 3, 19f., 37, 51, 78, 122

delivery 19–21, 73, 113, 127

democracy VIII, XIII, 1, 3, 5, 11, 16, 70, 81, 99, 113 f., 127, 129

Democratic Alliance (DA) XVI, 70–72, 113 f., 119

democratic consolidation XV, XVII, 1, 6, 23, 110, 129

democratic rights 16, 61, 81, 129

democratisation IX, XI–XIII, XVII, 9–12, 19, 24, 37, 95, 98, 107, 122 f.

demographic X, 8, 55, 67, 84, 98, 118

Department of Community Development 47

Department of Community Safety 54, 56

Department of Education 86

De Renzio, Paolo 2 f.

development VIII–XI, XIII, 1–4, 7–9, 12–15, 19–21, 24 f., 27–31, 33 f., 36, 38–40, 43–46, 48
     f., 51 f., 55, 58, 62, 64–66, 68 f., 71 f., 74, 77 f., 80, 86, 89, 92, 96, 102, 105, 111–115,
     117, 119 f., 122–125, 128, 130

Diani, Mario VIII, 11

H

I

J

K

L

Norwood Police Station 35 f., 55, 57, 59 f., 63, 88

Norwood Primary School 28

O

obligation 1, 5, 22 f., 26, 42, 53, 61, 81, 98 f., 101, 104, 112, 127

Offe, Claus 5, 9, 22, 81

opportunity VIII–XI, XIII, XVII, 1, 3 f., 6–9, 11 f., 14 f., 36, 43 f., 52 f., 74 f., 80 f., 87, 90 f., 93, 100, 102, 104–107, 110 f., 114, 116 f., 123, 126 f., 129

Orange Grove X–XII, XIV–XVI, 4, 19, 24, 26–28, 30 f., 34 f., 37 f., 46, 49, 57, 61, 63 f., 72, 75–78, 82–84, 86, 88 f., 91, 97, 99, 108, 111, 116 f., 119, 124 f., 128

Orange Grove Primary School 28, 84

Orange Grove Residents' Association (OGRA) XV, 34, 61, 63, 72, 116, 124, 128

P

Parent-Teacher Association (PTA) 82, 86

partnership 19, 63

Paterson Park 34–36, 45 f., 55, 72, 83, 85, 89, 111, 115 f., 119 f., 126

Paterson Park Development 72

Paterson Park Recreation Centre 35 f., 45 f., 55, 72, 111, 116, 120

patronage 7, 19, 21, 51, 59, 102

Pentecostal Church 32, 46, 97

Pieterse, Edgar XI, 12, 19

police 17 f., 36, 41, 46, 53, 55–63, 66, 78, 84, 88, 109, 117 f., 125

Police Services 58

political space 5

political trust 6, 22, 52, 78, 128

poor 2, 15 f., 19, 39 f., 44, 50, 52, 60, 63, 68, 77 f. 84, 89, 102 f., 105, 109, 113, 118, 125, 129, 130

Portes, Alejandro 2 f., 7 f., 74, 96

post-apartheid VIII, 3, 39 f., 49–51, 91, 95, 106, 110, 127, 130

poverty XII f., XV, 2, 4, 12, 15, 17, 19, 40, 77 f., 103, 105 f., 109 f., 114, 119–121, 124 f., 127, 129

power VIII–XI, XIII–XV, XVII, 1, 3–5, 7, 9, 11, 14 f., 17, 19 f., 23 f., 37, 39, 48, 50, 52, 68, 77, 79, 104, 109, 111 f., 114, 119, 123–127

prejudice X, 8, 15, 18, 30, 40, 103, 108

Presbyterian Church 100

priority 105

social dynamic X f., XIII–XV, XVII, 1, 4, 6, 39, 52, 120

social hierarchy 26

social movement VIII, 20 f.

social network VIII f., XII, 1, 5, 7–9, 11, 17, 22, 24, 49, 52, 62, 68, 70, 73 f., 76, 81, 112, 118, 126, 128, 130

social organisation XVII, 3, 5, 14, 49, 62, 77, 111, 128

social structure VIII f., XIV, 5, 10, 23, 44, 49 f., 55 f., 62, 65, 69, 74, 77, 82, 92, 95 f., 104, 112, 122, 126

socio-economic X, 3, 11 f., 15–17, 20, 38, 50, 52, 68, 70, 80 f., 84, 91, 106, 112, 114, 118, 126, 129

solidarity IX, 8, 18, 53, 62, 74, 95 f., 105, 109 f.

South Africa VIII–X, XII–XVII, 1–9, 11–18, 20 f., 23, 25, 28 f., 39 f., 45, 47, 49–51, 53, 58, 62, 69, 75–77, 80 f., 83, 88, 91, 95, 97 f., 100, 104, 106 f., 110 f., 114, 117–119, 121–123, 126 f., 129 f.

South African Communist Party (SACP) 12, 14 f.

Soweto Uprising 83

space IX–XI, XIII, XV–XVII, 1, 3 f., 7, 9, 12, 24, 27, 33–35, 39 f., 42, 44 f., 50 f., 55, 62, 68 f., 80, 96 f., 107, 112, 116, 120, 123 f., 128

space of agency 1, 3 f., 12, 50, 80, 123 f., 128

standard X f., 6, 11, 22, 26, 30, 39 f., 52, 66, 90 f., 95–98, 107, 110, 121, 124 f., 127

state VIII, X f., XIV, XVI f., 1–6, 8 f., 11–14, 17–23, 39 f., 43, 48–53, 65, 68, 70, 72, 76–78, 89, 91, 98, 104, 107–110, 112, 119, 121–125, 127–130

state capacity XI, XVII, 6, 9, 21, 39, 48, 109, 112, 122, 125, 128

status IX, 8, 17 f., 81, 88, 101, 111

Steyn, Melissa IX

Stolle, Dietlind 6, 8, 23, 52

structure IX, XII–XIV, XVI f., 1–3, 9, 11, 13, 15 f., 35, 40, 43–45, 47, 49–51, 55 f., 58, 69 f., 72, 75–77, 81 f., 86 f., 90, 92, 95, 98, 101, 104, 106, 119 f., 123, 125, 127, 129 f.

surveillance XV, 64

Suttner, Raymond 13 f.

systemic IX, XV, XVII, 1 f., 4, 16, 106, 123, 130

T

taxi 56–58

Taylor, Vivienne IX, 11

Terreblanche, Sampie 14–16

The Star 25, 28, 57